· WARD LOCK MASTER GARDENER ·

Fruit and Vegetable Clinic

PIPPA GREENWOOD

WARD LOCK

First published in Great Britain in 1993
by Ward Lock Limited, Villiers House, 41/47 Strand,
London WC2N 5JE, England
A Cassell Imprint

British Library Cataloguing in Publication Data
is available upon application to the British Library

ISBN 0 7063 7104 6

Text filmset by DP Press, Sevenoaks, England
Printed and bound in Singapore

Previous page: **When trained
against a wall an apple may
be grown in a fairly small
space and yet still produce
a good crop.**

Contents

Preface

However small your garden, you really should be able to find the space to grow some fruit and vegetables and, if possible, a few herbs too. More and more gardeners, of all levels of expertise, are developing an interest in home-grown produce. Some have large areas devoted to elaborate kitchen gardens, others have well stocked and meticulously planned allotments, and many more have typical back-yard gardens. But all have realized just how much pleasure growing your own food can bring! It may be that you like to grow less readily available crops, or that you like to know that you are eating wonderfully fresh and tender produce; you may even have realized that by 'doing it yourself' you can save a lot of money; and at the same time you can get enormous satisfaction from seeing your very own fruit and vegetables enjoyed by your family and friends.

But, however well you grow your plants, there will sometimes be problems with pests, diseases and disorders. With the help of this book, hopefully these will become something you can cope with. The book has been divided into chapters which should make it easy to find the information you need quickly. Whatever the crop, it is much less likely to succumb to diseases if it is grown well and in a suitable spot and, of course, if you always practise good garden hygiene. Chapter 2 provides plenty of helpful suggestions for avoiding trouble and throughout the other chapters you will find tips on preventing the build-up of specific pests and diseases.

Generally speaking, it is a combination of good gardening and careful use of chemicals which will provide you with the healthiest and heaviest crop. The range of chemicals available is constantly changing, so in addition to referring to the chart on page 94, it is worth keeping an eye open to see when the new products are produced. Throughout the text, the active or chemical ingredients of pesticides which can currently be used to control each pest or disease has been given. To complement this you will find a comprehensive chart on page 94 which indicates the proprietary names under which these chemicals are being sold. Whenever you use a chemical it is important to follow all the manu-facturer's instructions carefully, but for some general tips on safe and effective use of chemicals turn to Chapter 7.

Seedsmen and plant breeders are constantly producing new and upgraded fruit and vegetables for us to grow, and combine this with the huge range of fertilizers, composts and garden chemicals now available, and the aid of this book, you can look forward to many happy and productive hours growing fruit and vegetables.

P.G.

◀ A conference pear, grown as an espalier, forms an attractive yet productive screen.

ACKNOWLEDGEMENTS

The publishers are grateful to the following for grant-
ing permission to reproduce the following colour
photographs: Pat Brindley, pp. 1, 4, 12 and 52; Harry
Smith Horticultural Photographic Collection, pp. 8, 9, 16
(bottom), 21 *(all)*, 25 *(top)*, 41 *(top)*, 57, 61, 69 and 85 *(all)*;
Photos Horticultural Picture Library, pp. 13, 16 *(top)*, 17,
20, 24, 28, 29, 41 *(bottom)*, 44, 45, 49, 53 *(top)*, 56, 60, 64,
68, 72, 73, 76, 77 *(both)*; Royal Horticultural Society,
Wisley, p. 25 *(bottom)*; National Institute of Agricultural
Botany, p. 32 *(both)*; Central Science Laboratory, pp. 36,
40 and 53 *(bottom)*; Horticultural Research Inter-
national, Littlehampton, p. 81; and *Amateur Gardening*
magazine, pp. 88, 92 and 93.

The line drawings were drawn by Vana Haggerty F.L.S.
and Nils Solberg.

·1·
What is a Kitchen Garden?

It was the French who introduced the 'potager' where real care was taken to plant fruit, vegetables and herbs in a way which was not only productive but also attractive. But in Britain it was during the eighteenth and nineteenth centuries that kitchen gardens became very popular.

As the methods of growing tended to be very labour intensive, kitchen gardens were most common in the larger gardens owned by the very wealthy. Many of these gardens were walled, so allowing much fan or cordon-trained fruit to be grown, but in addition common features included hotbeds (where beds were created on levelled heaps of manure and the heat given off by this allowed early or out-of-season crops to be produced). The walls were sometimes heated too, by using internal flues, so allowing more tender fruit to be grown, or increasing the potential for prolonging natural growing seasons. In order to maximize the productivity of the kitchen garden, intercropping was always practised, and indeed to this day many gardeners use this technique to make best use of the space available!

Greenhouses were often included in kitchen gardens too and the Victorians became keen growers of some of the more exotic or tropical crops. The main cultivated areas were the beds and these were usually about 1.2 m (4 ft) wide, interspersed with paths. These served two main purposes: to provide easy access for the gardeners so that all the sowing, weeding and maintenance could be carried out easily; and also to allow owners of the property to keep an eye on things and even show off this well cultivated and attractive area to their house guests!

The modern kitchen garden
Nowadays a kitchen garden can be just as large or as small as you need it, with varying areas devoted to growing your favourite edible crops – fruit, vegetables and herbs. The more you can sensibly cram in the better, so if there are any walls or fences on its boundaries, use them to their full potential and try growing cordon, espalier or fan-trained fruit. With careful planning you can produce your own tasty fruit and vegetables for many months of the year, choosing different varieties to prolong the natural seasons of each crop as long as possible. The potential is huge and, if you want to add a few ornamentals in amongst the crop plants, do so for you will not only add interest and colour but also encourage plenty of useful visiting insects. Even if your garden is quite small, a mini-kitchen garden is still well worth the effort. The right selection of plants which will grow and crop well will add a new dimension to gardening and five-star quality to your meals!

Allotment gardening
If you're short of space and have a bit of spare time, it's well worth considering taking on an allotment.

◄ A small vegetable plot can be fitted into a garden of almost any size. The addition of a greenhouse further increases the range of crops you can raise and grow yourself.

► Most local authorities still provide allotments for a reasonable fee. There may be a waiting list, but your own allotment is something well worth the wait.

All you need to do is contact your local council to see what they have to offer. The terms and conditions will vary, as will the cost, but I'm sure you'll find it a good and very reasonable investment.

Allotment gardening seems to be more popular in some areas than in others so it is impossible to say whether they will have one available immediately or whether you will have to join a waiting list. If you do take one on, you will no doubt have to put in quite a bit of work but your efforts will be well rewarded. The size of allotments varies, but a rectangular 27 m (90 ft) by 9 m (30 ft) plot is the sort of thing to expect. You will find that this extra space provides you with room enough to experiment with a wider range of crops and growing methods and so will greatly expand not only the amount of food you produce during each season, but also your knowledge and skills.

For the less experienced there is also plenty to be learned and not just by trial and error – neighbouring allotment holders are a well known and very useful source of information, advice, help and encouragement.

The value of home-grown produce

There is nothing to beat home-grown fruit and vegetables. In terms of freshness, even the best local greengrocer with the fastest turnover cannot provide you with food so fresh. This means that everything from a French bean to a marrow has the best possible texture and taste; and of course its nutritional value is at its highest as there has been no chance for the produce to start deteriorating. You can pick it as you need it, in exactly the right quantities (allowing, of course, for the fact that as it tastes so wonderful everyone tends to eat more than you would expect!)

If you choose your varieties carefully and grow early or late crops, you can also save a lot of money and have plentiful supplies of vegetables and even some fruits when they are not at their cheapest in the shops. When it comes to choosing varieties to sow or plant, there is another big advantage in the range of crops you can grow. The choice in the greengrocer or supermarket is rather predictable and, dare I say it, a bit limited – what we get offered is generally what the farmers and growers can produce most easily. This is usually the variety which crops reliably and which produces the sort of even-sized, even-shaped, attractive (but perhaps not so tasty) crops the supermarkets seem to like to stock. If you grow your own you have a huge range to choose from and almost certainly you will find you prefer what you choose to what is more easily available in the shops!

There will no doubt be times when you produce gluts of one crop or another, but use this to your advantage – enjoy a feast, freeze some for later in the year and remember your friends and relatives who would probably love some really fresh produce.

Last, but certainly not least, there is the tremendous sense of achievement when your very own fruit and vegetables start to develop and then are ready to eat.

· 2 ·
Good Gardening

Good gardening not only means a much better crop and more vigorous plants which crop for longer; most importantly, it can also save you a lot of time and heartache! Any healthy plant which is growing well is less prone to attack by diseases and pests and, even if it does succumb, will be better equipped to compensate for the damage by producing new growth. But good gardening is not just about nurturing individual plants, it also means keeping the area around each plant free of weeds and debris. This makes the garden look better and also helps to remove the sources of many diseases, and the hiding places of many pests. Where appropriate, pruning is also important because, if it is carried out well, it can help to keep the crown of the plant open – often deterring diseases – and will remove sources of overwintering pests and diseases.

If your fruit and vegetables suffer attacks of diseases or pests, it is important to remove affected parts of the plant as soon as possible; and to remove any fallen leaves which may harbour the problem.

Feeding and watering

Without an adequate supply of both food and water plants may not only give a very disappointing crop, they could even die. There are very few garden soils which have serious nutrient deficiencies but, for the best possible performance, you may need to top up levels of specific nutrients, or to apply a complete fertilizer.

If growing conditions are not ideal, symptoms of nutrient deficiency can develop on plants because, even if the soil contains plenty of nutrients, they may not be in an available form or the plant may not be able to take them up. Soils which are too dry, or waterlogged, may make it impossible for the plants to obtain all they need, so correct levels of watering are absolutely essential. Deficiencies of calcium – responsible for causing bitter pit of apples, and blossom end rot of peppers and tomatoes – are largely the result of erratic and inadequate watering. Regular watering also helps to prevent uneven growth which may cause small, distorted crops or cracks and splits in stems.

When it comes to feeding, the correct timing is important so that the plant can gain maximum benefit and not be encouraged to put on growth at a time when it will then be subjected to extremes of weather. The type of fertilizer should also be selected carefully as, for example, excessive levels of potash can cause deficiencies of magnesium, while excessive use of high nitrogen feeds may cause a plant to produce growth which is very soft – this may sound good, but in reality it also makes it more susceptible to attack by many pests and diseases!

Light

Plenty of light is needed to allow plants to produce energy by the process called photosynthesis. Water from the soil and carbon dioxide gas from the air are also needed but, if light or any of these other factors are lacking, then the whole process comes to a halt. Without any light the foliage soon turns yellow and the stems become elongated, spindly and weak, and the plant gradually deteriorates.

If there is too much shade then, although the plant will probably survive, the chances of it producing a worthwhile crop are very slim. Poor light levels often lead to very poor flowering and with woody plants like tree and bush fruits, sun is needed to ripen the wood and ensure that plenty of flower buds are produced.

Once the fruits are formed, sun is again vital to give the crop that delicious sweet flavour and strong colour we all crave. Adequate sunlight is particularly important for dessert fruits as these have a much higher sugar content than the culinary varieties.

As different plants have different light requirements, choose planting sites carefully so that the crops will have enough light at all stages in their development: save south-facing positions for the crops which really need it, and perhaps try the hardier and culinary fruits in the less sunny spots. Always check the growing requirements stated on the back of seed packets. Light is needed for germination of some seeds and, once in the ground, some vegetables will need more light than others.

Temperature and weather

Most plants can survive under quite wide-ranging temperature and weather regimes, but they may not thrive and crop well. At either temperature extremes the life processes will be disrupted: growth will be affected and cells may rupture as a

◄ 'Morello' cherries are often trained on a shaded wall – providing a beautiful display of blossom, followed by lush dark, glossy fruits.

► If you have sufficient space, a great range of fruits can be grown spanning the length of the cropping season and even providing fruit for storage.

result of frost and very low temperatures, or be scorched when temperatures rise greatly. Each plant will have its own temperature and weather preferences, so check particular needs and requirements before deciding what to plant and where to plant it. It may seem disappointing not to be able to grow one particular plant, but it is better to face the facts and to stick to what will work!

High temperatures may cause a range of different problems and symptoms – from the 'side effects' such as water shortage to the direct effects such as the development of brown patches on foliage or fruits. Low temperatures are renowned for the damage caused by frosts, where parts of plants or whole plants may be killed. If the blossom of, say, a plum tree is subjected to frost, however wonderful the weather is for the rest of the year, you'll still be lucky if you get any fruit!

· STORAGE TIME FOR VEGETABLE SEEDS ·

Whenever you buy a packet of seed you usually find that it contains far more seed than you could conceivably use in a single season. Provided you keep the packets in a cool, dry place the seeds of almost all vegetables remain viable for at least a year. The figures given below are conservative estimates – if you are prepared to accept lower germination levels, their storage time can be longer:

Vegetable seed	Number of years	Vegetable seed	Number of years
Asparagus	3	Melon	5
Beans (French, runner)	3	Onion	1
Beetroot	4	Parsley	2
Broccoli	5	Parsnip	1
Brussels sprout	5	Pea	3
Cabbage	4	Radish	5
Carrot	3	Salsify	2
Cauliflower	4	Scorzonera	2
Celery	5	Spinach	5
Cucumber	5	Sweet corn	1
Leek	3	Sweet pepper	4
Lettuce	4	Tomato	4
Marrow	5	Turnip	5

Extremes in rainfall can also be very damaging, leading either to symptoms of drought or water-logging. A particularly hard rainfall can even lead to damage of the leaves and fruits.

To a large extent there is nothing much we can do about prevailing weather conditions, but it is worth considering erecting protective barriers such as windbreaks, or insulating beds or individual plants with spun polypropylene fleece to protect against low temperatures.

Crop rotation

Crop rotation is a very efficient way of ensuring that you keep soil-borne diseases and pests to a minimum. The idea, quite simply, is that the positions of crops are changed every year so that before pests and diseases have time to build up to damaging levels on one spot, you will have planted a new, unrelated crop which is not susceptible. It ensures that there is less likelihood of nutrient deficiencies developing: each type of crop will have slightly different requirements, while at the same time allowing you to cater for first one crop which likes a very rich and newly manured site, followed by a different crop which prefers lower levels of nutrients.

Crop rotation is only really practical for annual crops. The rotation usually works on a three-year basis. Occasionally a four-year rotation is used, but for the purposes of this book I will stick to the more commonly used three-year plan (Fig. 1).

The area in which you grow your vegetables needs to be divided into three sections. You need to consider the vegetables you want to grow as belonging to one of the following groups:

● *Root crops/potatoes* including parsnips, carrots, salsify, scorzonera, beetroot and parsley. Also potatoes and tomatoes (because they are closely related to potatoes).

● *Brassicas* including cabbage, cauliflower, Brussels sprouts, kale, broccoli, calabrese, Chinese cabbage (and most of the other similar oriental vegetables which have become available recently), kohl rabi, turnip, swede and radish.

● *Peas and onions* including peas, sugar snap peas, mange tout, runner beans, dwarf French beans, climbing French beans and broad beans. Also onions, shallots, leeks, chives and garlic.

On any one plot in any one year you can, of course, grow just one or a combination of several of the vegetables mentioned in one group. Then rotate them according to the following type of pattern:

	First Year	Second Year	Third Year
Section 1	Potatoes/roots	Peas/onions	Brassicas
Section 2	Brassicas	Potatoes/roots	Peas/onions
Section 3	Peas/onions	Brassicas	Potatoes/roots

If this all sounds like a lot of hard work, remember it is a practice which has been used successfully by farmers (and gardeners!) for centuries. It will help to control many common plant problems, including parsnip canker, violet

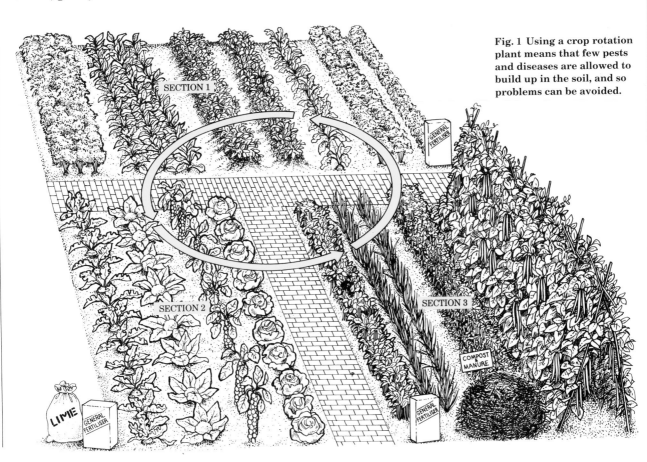

Fig. 1 Using a crop rotation plant means that few pests and diseases are allowed to build up in the soil, and so problems can be avoided.

root rot, potato cyst eelworm, potato blight and powdery scab, club root, white blister, foot and root rots and wilts (especially troublesome on peas and beans), anthracnose, leek rust, stem and bulb eelworm of onions, white rot and smut of onions and related crops. So you can see, it really is well worth using rotation, even if your vegetable plot is only quite small!

Weeding

Weeding is one aspect of gardening which seems to make almost everyone groan. It is not that it is hard physical work – on the contrary, it is probably one of the lighter jobs – but it is just that it seems to go on and on… and on. During the height of the season, particularly if there has been good warm weather and a fair amount of rain, conditions are perfect for tremendous weed growth.

▲ Annual weeds may be hoed off or, if the area is to be dug over they may be incorporated, but do this before they set seed.

► If left to grow unchecked weeds soon take over, so regular control is essential.

◄ Polythene sheeting makes an inexpensive mulch which is simple to use and helps keep the soil moist and weed free.

Weeds can cause a lot of problems in amongst your crops. To begin with they may harbour pests and diseases so that even if you regularly check and spray your crops, there is always a new source of the problem waiting close by to re-invade! They may also allow problems to overwinter, so that even if you think you have done a brilliant job at cleaning up the end of the season, again the problem is ready and waiting as soon as the new crop is growing. Weeds can also provide tremendous competition as they use up vast quantities of water and nutrients because they grow so rapidly. Once growing strongly, they may swamp your crops and so compete for light too. Finally, the very presence of weeds around your plants will tend to encourage humid, still air which is just the sort of environment many diseases really thrive in.

The methods you choose to control weeds could include hand pulling, hoeing, mulching (to deprive the weeds of light and air) and, where possible, weedkillers. Prompt action is the key to success: many weeds seed very rapidly and have extremely efficient methods of dispersal – some even producing the equivalent of three generations in a single year! Always remove as much of the weed as possible – the roots of many pernicious perennials like dandelions, if broken into several pieces, will actually form a new plant from each piece!

When it comes to composting, remember the old saying 'if in doubt, leave it out' – many weeds (or their seeds) survive the composting process and so it really is safest to leave them all out and confine them to the bin!

Location

Choosing the site on which to grow your crops is fundamentally important, as it can literally mean the difference between success and failure. The rate at which a plant grows and develops, and its ability to produce a good crop, are influenced by many factors, several of which are directly linked with the growing site. Soil is potentially variable, so always check that the site you have in mind for each particular crop has the right sort of texture: that it is neither too light nor too heavy, drains neither too fast nor too slow, and of course has the right pH (level of acidity). Not all these factors will affect all plants but the particular preferences of fruit and vegetables can always be found either in a reference book, or on the back of the seed pack.

Some plants need a lot more sun and warmer temperatures than others and there will even be differences in their tolerance of frost and wind. This, too, needs to be thought about carefully before you decide what to plant and where.

Planting

Even the healthiest, most vigorous plant with the best possible potential can be completely wasted if it is not planted properly. It can even be killed.

Planting includes the preparation of the site or planting hole, as well as the act of putting the plant in the ground. The precise needs and best method for each plant will vary, but there are a few ground rules which are always worth bearing in mind:

● Make sure the soil has been dug over well before planting so that it has a good and even texture – break down large clods of earth, remove large stones, buried rubble etc.

● Incorporate organic matter. This improves both light, sandy soils as well as heavy, sticky ones.

● Incorporate a fertilizer (organic or chemical).

● In heavy soils, avoid creating a sump effect by making a small planting hole and filling it with bulky material – this tends to draw the water in from the surrounding soil and so causes waterlogging.

● When planting, remember that the roots and only the roots were created to go underground – if you bury stems or trunks of anything from a seedling to a tree, it is likely to deteriorate and the plant may be killed.

● With bare root and container-grown plants, always spread the roots out well before planting – this will encourage balanced growth.

● Water in well newly planted crops.

● Finally, don't go away and forget your new plants – their establishment will be far more successful if you continue to nurture them.

Pruning (Fig. 2)

Pruning, if carried out properly and at the correct time of the year, can do a great deal towards producing a strong plant which gives a good crop. It can also help to keep the fruit on larger trees within your reach. It allows you to keep the crown of the plant fairly open so plenty of sunlight reaches the branches and developing fruits, and so that there is good air movement – most diseases thrive in stagnant air and many can be kept at bay, or at least at acceptable levels, if air circulation is improved.

Pruning should encourage fruiting and at the same time allow you to remove any straggly or unhealthy branches. All these wonderful benefits can be lost if a bad job is done and it is not unheard of for all the fruiting potential to be pruned out!

If in doubt as to the timing, method or extent of pruning needed, always check before starting.

Pollination

Pollination is, of course, vital for a good crop of fruit. Unfavourable weather or environmental conditions can reduce the efficiency and number of pollination insects: very cold spells or indeed very windy weather can drastically reduce their numbers – in unpleasant weather they too prefer to stay hidden away in sheltered spots, and in extreme weather they may even be killed. It is worth trying to create a certain amount of shelter around your vegetables and fruit to protect them against poor weather.

Unless all the flowers of a plant are pollinated, the amount of fruit set will obviously be reduced, and in some cases their shape and development is altered. On strawberries, for example, a small and distorted fruit may be formed, with each fruit having a rather tough texture.

With some crops – most commonly peaches and marrows – it is advisable to pollinate the flowers artificially using a soft paint brush (Fig. 3).

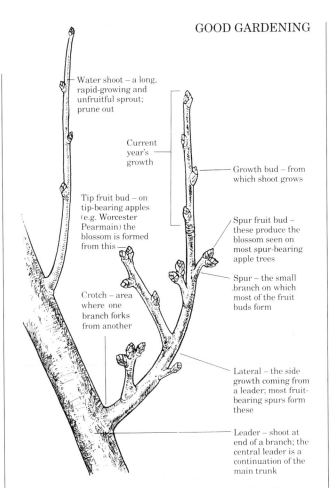

Water shoot – a long, rapid-growing and unfruitful sprout; prune out

Current year's growth

Tip fruit bud – on tip-bearing apples (e.g. Worcester Pearmain) the blossom is formed from this

Growth bud – from which shoot grows

Spur fruit bud – these produce the blossom seen on most spur-bearing apple trees

Spur – the small branch on which most of the fruit buds form

Crotch – area where one branch forks from another

Lateral – the side growth coming from a leader; most fruit-bearing spurs form these

Leader – shoot at end of a branch; the central leader is a continuation of the main trunk

Fig. 2 Pruning is an important technique to allow the optimum crop, whilst at the same time allowing unhealthy or weak growth to be removed.

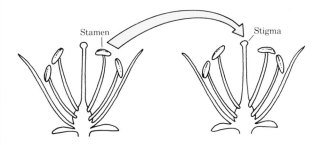

Stamen

Stigma

Fig. 3 Using an artist's soft paintbrush, carefully transfer pollen from the stamens of one flower to the stigma of another.

19

Diseases

Diseases can be caused by a wide range of organisms, the most common being fungi, viruses and bacteria. The pathogens responsible for causing the symptoms are often very small and, in the case of viruses, they cannot even be seen with the aid of a standard microscope. Nevertheless, the symptoms they cause can be devastating!

Diseases may attack any part of the plant, but usually any one problem appears only on certain areas. The symptoms produced vary but the growth, development and appearance of the plant are usually affected and some diseases may prove fatal. Some diseases spread very quickly and easily, others spread much more slowly, but all are infectious. The growing conditions and the weather often have a strong influence on disease spread and development.

Diseases are best controlled by a combination of good gardening and garden hygiene, prompt action (often using an appropriate fungicide – see page 94), and, where possible, the planting of resistant varieties for future crops.

Some disease-causing agents are spread by vectors – for example, aphids often carry and transmit viruses as they feed – and so the possibility of controlling the vector should also be investigated.

Pests

Pests come in a very wide range of types and forms and could be said to include insects, mites, molluscs (slugs and snails), as well as larger animals such as rabbits, mice and certain birds. Some of the insects and mites can only be seen with the aid of a microscope or hand lens, but in the main they are far larger and easier to see than most disease-causing organisms.

Pests are capable of attacking almost any part of a plant, but individually they tend to be restricted to one or only a few specific areas.

The type of damage done varies greatly too, and is often determined by the way in which the pest feeds: there may be holes gnawed, grazed or chewed, puckering and distortion as a result of sap-sucking pests. Occasionally a whole plant may be eaten, but generally some parts are left behind. Some pests feed underground and, if they attack the plant roots, this may go un-noticed until the whole plant starts to deteriorate and die.

Pest attacks are very likely to spread, as the culprits involved are usually mobile and can quickly walk, fly or crawl from one part of a plant to another, and from one host to the next.

With insect pests, control is usually best achieved by a combination of good gardening, removal of the pests by hand (where feasible) and, where necessary, the use of proprietary insecticides (see page 94).

◄ Snails come in many colours and sizes but all need to be controlled.

► Gooseberry sawfly larvae rapidly reduce the leaves to skeletons.

▼ Blackfly on broad beans look unsightly and can be very damaging.

► Mealy cabbage aphids are often clustered together beneath the leaf.

Disorders

Plant disorders are not infectious and so they will not spread or be spread within the crop and, however hard you search there is no 'culprit' to be seen. The appearance of an 'outbreak' can, however, be given when several plants are affected by the disorder and when some succumb after others.

Disorders are commonly caused by unsuitable growing or environmental conditions, or by deficiencies of vital nutrients. The weather and growing conditions may also cause disorders indirectly, by influencing the availability of certain nutrients or the plant's ability to take them up.

Disorders may cause permanent damage but, generally speaking, they can be avoided and the development of further symptoms prevented by improving the growing conditions and/or correct feeding to ensure that the plant has the best chance in its chosen environment.

Resistance

Always seek out plants which are resistant to problems commonly found in the garden. A plant which is resistant may show a complete or partial ability to resist attack by a named pest or disease. There are relatively few plants available which show pest resistance; the majority are disease resistant. Just because it is resistant to one problem does not, however, mean it will not be attacked by others.

Resistance may break down under certain conditions but, generally speaking, a plant or variety sold as resistant is worth its weight in gold because it should, under most conditions, grow away without suffering from that particular problem. If you cannot find varieties sold as resistant to the problem you have in mind, then it is always worth working from your own experience and that of friends.

· RESISTANT VEGETABLE VARIETIES ·	
Vegetables and their varieties	**Resistant to**
Brussels sprout 'Cor', 'Rampart'	Leaf spot Powdery mildew White blister
Carrot 'Nandor', 'Nantucket', 'Sytan'	Some resistance to carrot root fly
Cucumber 'Bush Champion', 'Petita'	Cucumber mosaic virus
Leek 'Autumn Mammoth'/'Walton Mammoth', 'Gernnevilliers-Splendid', 'Titan'	Rust
Lettuce 'Avon defiance', 'Musette', 'Sabine'	Root aphids Downy mildew
Marrow/courgette 'Supremo', 'Tiger Cross'	Cucumber mosaic virus
Parsnip 'Avonresister', 'Cobham Improved', 'Gladiator', 'White Gem'	Canker
Potato 'Cara', 'Estima', 'Maris Peer', 'Pentland Crown', 'Pentland Ivory', 'Pentland Squire', 'Romana', 'Wilja'	Potato blight
'Arran Comet', 'Arran Pilot', 'Golden Wonder', 'King Edward', 'Maris Peer', 'Pentland Crown', 'Pentland Javelin'	Powdery scab
'Home Guard', 'Romano', 'Ulster Chieftan'	Spraing
Tomato 'Cumulus', 'Estrella', 'Piranto', 'Seville Cross', 'Shirley'	Leaf mould some viruses foot and root rots/wilts
'Cherry Wonder', 'Estella', 'Eurocross BB' 'Money Maker', 'Seville Cross'	Greenback

· 3 ·

Vegetable Clinic

It is very disappointing when the vegetables you have nurtured so carefully are attacked by pests or diseases. Like any plant they are susceptible to a range of problems at almost every stage of their development – but don't let this put you off because, with a little bit of effort, many of these setbacks can be avoided or controlled fairly easily. It's also worth bearing in mind that the damage caused by many pests and diseases may not significantly lower the crop which you harvest: for instance, leek rust may make the plants look terrible, but it is rarely found on anything other than the outer leaves, and these are usually discarded before the leek is cooked. If the pest or disease can be removed, it need not stop you eating the crop: a heavy infestation of aphids or caterpillars may build up frighteningly rapidly but both are easily removed from most vegetables and, provided you have been growing for your own use, a little bit of stunting or distortion, or a leaf of cabbage with the odd hole in it, is not something you need be too worried about. The real difficulty arises when you are growing for exhibitions or shows, and then only perfect produce really is the order of the day!

Many gardeners are happy to use garden chemicals on ornamental plants and shrubs, but when it comes to spraying vegetables they are more wary. Provided you choose a chemical which carries a label recommendation for use on the type of plant you plan to use it on, and provided you use it exactly according to the manufacturer's instructions, it should be perfectly safe. The 'harvest interval', or amount of time you must wait between applying the chemical and eating the vegetable, must be observed too.

The need to treat with chemicals can be kept to a minimum if you always ensure that your vegetables are grown well and if you use non-chemical methods such as spun polypropylene fleece to prevent the pests getting the chance to attack or lay their eggs in the first place. Varieties of vegetables may also be on sale which have been bred to show resistance to attack by any pest or disease which is particularly troublesome in your garden or allotment. It is definitely worth looking through the current seed catalogues to see what is available. Even if the crop still suffers some attack, the overall effect will be much better.

In this chapter you will find helpful information on identifying, avoiding and controlling some of the more common problems which you may come across on your vegetables. Where chemicals are mentioned too, you should refer to the chart on page 94 for details of brand names.

SALAD VEGETABLES

Beetroot

● *Leaf miner* grubs tunnel within the leaf and a yellow blotch mine develops. This turns brown and dry with a papery texture, and if you hold the

◄ Crops with tender foliage and growing close to the ground are a particularly easy target for slugs.

leaf up to the light you should be able to see the plump maggots within the mines. Mostly symptoms are first noticed between late spring and early autumn, but it is not usually of significance except on young plants, which may be stunted if severely attacked early on.

○ Pick off affected leaves and destroy them so that the maggots are killed. The pupae overwinter in the soil, so regular and frequent cultivation helps to reduce numbers for next year as they will be eaten by birds.

Celery

● *Heart rot* is caused by a bacterium that makes the centre of the celery turn brown, slimey and often foul-smelling. It may spread from the heart up the stalks and the whole plant is soon ruined.

○ The bacteria enter the celery through wounds so try to minimize injury caused by slugs and snails etc. Always earth up very carefully and avoid hoeing too close to the plants. Protect from frost, which may cause cracking. Remove affected plants as there is no control available.

● *Leaf miners* cause pale green patches to develop on the celery foliage as the larvae of the celery fly tunnel within it. Each patch turns dry and brown. These mines may look like patches of scorched foliage or disease, but the maggots responsible may be visible if the leaf is held up to the light. There are two generations a year: the first appears between mid-spring and early summer and may do significant damage by stunting the growth of the young plants and causing the development of celery sticks with a stringy texture and poor taste; the second generation arrives in mid-summer and, although more mines are produced at this time of year, the crop is usually affected less.

○ Remove affected leaves and destroy them so that the maggots are killed. Spray with malathion.

▲ Asparagus beetles and
their larvae feed on stems
and foliage of asparagus
and may cause die back.

◄ Celery leaf miner maggots
attack the foliage of celery
and parsnips and may stunt
a young plant's growth.

Cucumber

● *Cucumber mosaic virus* is a common problem on courgettes, marrows and many ornamentals. Affected plants are stunted and their leaves distorted and covered in yellow blotches and contrasting dark green patches. The virus is easily spread by aphids as they feed, so control these pests. It may also be spread by handling, and on tools, so handle affected plants last and clean tools thoroughly.

○ There is no cure and affected plants should be destroyed. Raise several extra plants each year so you can have replacements ready.

● *Foot and root rots* are caused by a range of microscopic fungi. Leaves of the cucumber start to discolour and gradually the whole plant withers and dies. The symptoms usually appear on the older leaves first and the base of the stem may become visibly blackened.

○ Remove affected plants. Use clean compost and containers (or fresh greenhouse border soil) and only mains water. The problem is if there are several plants growing in the border or growing bag, as the chances are that they will all become affected because the fungi are easily moved around in soil water.

● *Powdery mildew* can be seen as white or pale grey powdery deposits of fungal spores on the foliage and may cause it to distort slightly and to wither and die. The stems may be attacked too. If the plants are dry at the roots then powdery mildew is likely to be especially troublesome, so keep the plants adequately watered. Moist air around the foliage often encourages the disease too, so try to improve air circulation.

○ Pick off affected leaves. Spray affected plants with a fungicide containing carbendazim, benomyl or other suitable fungicide.

> **· HANDY TIP ·**
>
> If virus diseases are a problem, don't hesitate to remove and burn the affected plants. The virus particles are present within all areas of the plant, so removal of obviously affected leaves is not enough. Ensure aphids and other sap-feeding pests are controlled too as these often spread viruses.

● *Withering* is most likely to be the result of poor growing conditions such as low temperatures, inadequate feeding or overwatering. Most frustratingly, withering starts just as the cucumber begins to form young fruits.

○ Pick off affected fruits as they will not develop normally and are simply putting added strain on the plant. Later fruits should develop normally if you remove all those which start to show signs of withering and then concentrate on good feeding and maintenance.

Lettuce

● *Cutworms* are caterpillars which feed underground, chewing at the lettuce roots and sometimes severing the stems at ground level (Fig. 4). Even if they do not kill the plants, the damage they cause allows the entry of diseases which can prove fatal. Cutworms are a creamy brown colour and up to 4 cm ($1^3/_4$ in) in length. Affected plants are stunted and soon die.

○ Collect up and dispose of the caterpillars. Cultivate regularly to expose the caterpillars to birds. Treat the soil with phoxim, chlorpyrifos and diazinon or other soil pesticide before planting.

● *Downy mildew* causes the older leaves to develop pale, discoloured patches, each of which corresponds with a white, fuzzy, fungal growth on the undersurface. Seedlings are frequently

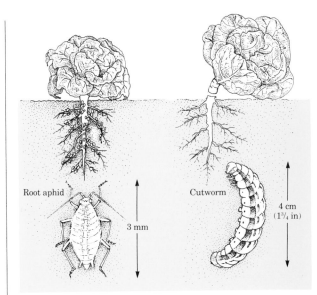

Fig. 4 Cut worm and root aphid are two common pests of lettuce. The damage they cause to the roots causes poor leaf growth.

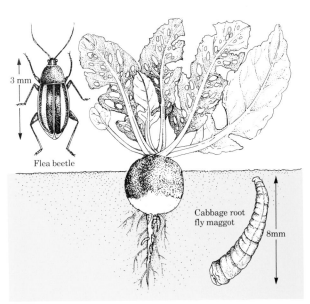

Fig. 5 Root fly maggots attack the roots of seedlings and mature radishes, preventing normal growth. Flea beetles eat holes in the foliage – seedlings are especially prone.

affected. The fungus thrives in moist places, so encourage good air circulation by keeping plants well spaced, and weed regularly.

○ Remove affected leaves and spray with mancozeb. Grow resistant varieties.

● *Root aphid* symptoms are usually seen in hot weather when the lettuces seem to grow very slowly and wilt, even if supplied with plenty of water. The aphids suck sap from the roots so if you lift a plant you will see clusters of these white, almost waxy-looking pests (Fig. 4).

○ Remove affected plants, keep the remainder well watered and drench them with malathion. Grow lettuces on a new site and choose resistant varieties (see page 22).

Radish

● *Cabbage root fly* maggots tunnel into the roots as they swell and chew at the young roots (Fig. 5). Radishes sown between mid-spring and late summer are especially prone.

○ No control is available but plants can be protected by fitting each with a flexible collar of carpet underlay or proprietary brassica collar.

● *Flea beetle* adults, up to 3 mm long and striped black and yellow or pure black feed on the leaves and cause small holes to appear (Fig. 5). They are easy to recognize because if you disturb them, they leap into the air. Keep radishes well watered and fed and they should be little affected by the damage. Young plants may suffer stunting.

○ Chemical control is not usually necessary but derris could be used.

Tomato (Fig. 6)

● *Blossom end rot* develops as a sunken black leathery patch on the flower end of the fruit. This is caused by inadequate or irregular watering

which causes a deficiency of calcium within the fruits, so plants in pots or growing bags are frequently affected. A low pH of the growing medium may also encourage this disorder.
❍ Regular watering is essential, together with good cultivation to ensure that a vigorous root system develops.

● *Blotchy ripening* symptoms are similar to those of greenback, but the unripened patches are randomly scattered over the fruit's surface.
❍ Keep temperatures down and provide some shade and good air circulation.

● *Greenback* affects the shoulder area of the fruit which remains yellow or pale green and hard. This disorder is common in very hot, sunny periods, and if the plants are not supplied with adequate potash.
❍ Provide good ventilation and use shading on the greenhouse. Feed with special tomato fertilizer. Grow resistant varieties which should not succumb except in very hot conditions.

● *Magnesium deficiency* causes lower leaves to develop yellow and later brown patches between the veins. Younger leaves may be affected later. Tomatoes which are growing in compost of a low pH and are fed special tomato fertilizers are often affected.
❍ Spray every seven days with a solution containing 200 g (7 oz) Epsom salts in 10 litres (2¼ gal) of water. Add a few drops of soft soap or a mild liquid detergent to act as a 'wetter'. This disorder is not as serious as it looks.

● *Root rots* caused by a range of soil or water-borne microscopic fungi, attack the plant's roots or stem base and cause the foliage to discolour and the plant to become stunted and later wilt and die. Plants grown in pots or in soil in which tomatoes have been grown before are most susceptible. The

▲ Blossom end rot is common on tomatoes and sometimes on peppers, causing a dark, sunken patch at the blossom end.

▶ Greenhouse shading is essential to protect the plants from extremes of temperature and scorching from the sun.

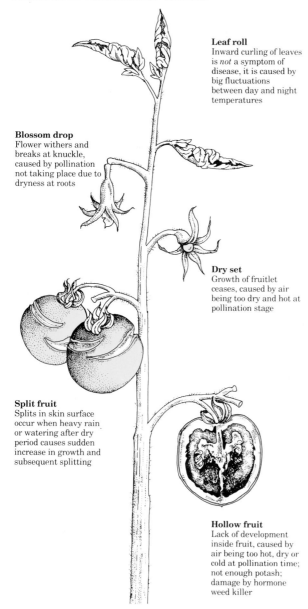

Leaf roll
Inward curling of leaves is *not* a symptom of disease, it is caused by big fluctuations between day and night temperatures

Blossom drop
Flower withers and breaks at knuckle, caused by pollination not taking place due to dryness at roots

Dry set
Growth of fruitlet ceases, caused by air being too dry and hot at pollination stage

Split fruit
Splits in skin surface occur when heavy rain or watering after dry period causes sudden increase in growth and subsequent splitting

Hollow fruit
Lack of development inside fruit, caused by air being too hot, dry or cold at pollination time; not enough potash; damage by hormone weed killer

Fig. 6 It is easy to produce an excellent crop of tomatoes but there is also a wide range of problems which may occur. A few examples are shown here; check carefully as the symptom may be on one part of the plant and the cause on another.

fungi are often introduced in water from butts, or if growing conditions are not adequately hygienic.
○ Use new, sterilized compost, or a fresh site and mains water. On seedlings drench with a copper-based fungicide.

● *Tomato blight* causes brown patches to appear on the foliage and stems, and in damp conditions a white fungal growth may be visible beneath. The fruits also develop brown patches and may rot on the plant. Some fruits appear healthy when picked but rot within a week of picking. It does not occur every year but, if moist, humid weather conditions prevail, it may have a devastating effect. Greenhouse-grown tomatoes are not usually affected.
○ Clean up all plant debris and grow on a new site next year. The same disease may attack potatoes so check and treat these too. Carefully spray with a copper-based fungicide or mancozeb from mid-summer.

● *Tomato leaf mould* rarely affects outdoor plants. A purplish-brown felty fungal growth develops on the lower leaf surface. The upper surface bears corresponding pale blotches. The fungus thrives in warm, humid conditions so ensure good air circulation and ventilation and keep temperatures below 21°C (70°F).
○ Spray with benomyl or mancozeb. Grow resistant varieties (see page 22).

● *Virus disease* symptoms include stunting, distortion, leaf puckering and yellow mosaic or blotch patterns on the foliage. Fruiting is poor or non-existent, but if fruits are produced they may be discoloured. Most viruses are spread by aphids or other sap-sucking pests, or by handling.
○ Control pests. Destroy infected plants. Never handle healthy plants after touching those which are infected or suspect.

TENDER VEGETABLES

Bean – dwarf, French, runner

● *Failure to set pod* can be the result of attacks by birds, or cold, wet weather making pollination impossible, but it is often caused by insufficient or erratic watering.

○ Sow runner beans in blocks in a sheltered spot to encourage pollinating insects. Water regularly and copiously from when the flower buds are seen. Incorporate plenty of bulky material into the trench before planting or sowing. Grow white or pink-flowered varieties as these seem less susceptible. Erect bird-scaring devices if necessary.

● *Foot and root rots* may develop from a range of soil-borne fungi, which rot the roots and stem bases, causing the plants to grow slowly, discolour and collapse (Fig. 7).

○ Grow beans on a fresh site each year. Remove affected plants.

● *Halo blight* causes leaves to develop angular spots, each surrounded by a bright yellow halo. This disease is often introduced on infected seed and the bacteria responsible are spread from leaf to leaf by water splash. Stems may show blotches which later turn a red-brown colour and ooze bacteria in wet conditions.

○ Remove affected leaves or whole plants and avoid overhead watering. Do not save seed.

Carrot

● *Carrot fly* have cream-coloured grubs, about 8 mm (1/4 in) long, which feed on the roots and then tunnel into the tap root, making it inedible. Foliage is discoloured and the plants grow slowly and wilt (Fig. 8). The pests overwinter as pupae in the soil, or in carrots left in the ground. Once the damage has been done, control is not likely to be effective.

○ Sow crops towards the end of spring or later, and harvest them before the end of summer. Surround

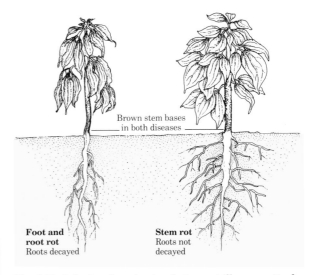

Fig. 7 Both foot and root rot and stem rot diseases attack the very base of the plant, causing the plant to discolour and rapidly collapse. However, whilst in foot and root rot the root system decays, in stem rot it does not.

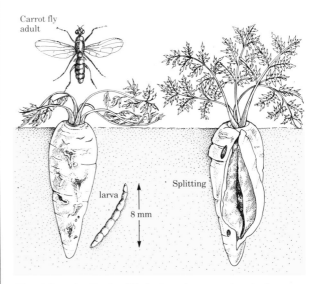

Fig. 8 Longitudinal splits in carrots suggest watering problems, so growing conditions should be improved. Tunnelling by the maggots of carrot fly causes a reddish-brown discolouration.

▲ Onion white rot may be devastating, causing rapid deterioration starting at the base of the bulbs.

◄ A fine mesh barrier or screen erected around the carrot crop is an effective means of preventing carrot fly attack.

the crop with a barrier of fine mesh or clear polythene, to about 90 cm (3 ft) above ground level, or lay horticultural fleece over it to prevent the adults from approaching the crop. Try to avoid injury to the carrot foliage as the smell emitted when the foliage is crushed attracts carrot flies. Use a soil insecticide such as phoxim or pirimiphos-methyl according to the manufacturer's instructions.

● *Splitting* – longitudinal splits in the tap root – is generally caused by erratic watering or heavy rainfall after a prolonged dry period (Fig. 8).
○ Keep the soil adequately moist at all times. Do not store affected carrots.

Marrow and courgette

● *Foot and root rots* caused by a range of soil-borne fungal pathogens, attack roots and stem base so the plant develops discoloured foliage and may wilt or collapse.
○ Grow marrows and courgettes on a fresh site. Clear up all debris at the end of the season.

● *Powdery mildew* develops as powdery white patches of fungal spores on the foliage and may cause it to die off.
○ Remove affected leaves and spray with a fungicide such as carbendazim or benomyl. Keep plants moist at the roots.

● *Viruses,* of which the most frequently involved is cucumber mosaic virus. Plants are stunted and the leaves distorted and blotched yellow. Fruit set is poor or non-existent but if they do form they are pitted, small, distorted and blotched yellow and dark green. Affected fruits are rather hard and not worth eating.
○ The virus is spread mainly by handling and by aphids, so minimize contact with the plants and spray against aphids (see page 94). Remove and burn affected plants. Do not save seed.

Onion, chive, garlic and shallot

● *Downy mildew* develops as yellowish blotches on affected foliage and these soon become covered in a dense felty fungal growth which is a purplish-brown colour. The leaves soon collapse, dying back from the tip and rapidly giving the onion plant the appearance of being dead. Wet, cool conditions encourage this disease.
○ Remove severely affected plants and spray those showing early symptoms with mancozeb. Remove all debris at the end of the season and practise crop rotation (see page 14).

● *Eelworm* are tiny, only 1–2 mm long, but cause severe distortion of the leaves. The base of the plant is excessively swollen and may split, which means that even if a bulb is formed, it cannot be stored and may become infected by secondary fungal organisms in the soil. Crop rotation may help to prevent plants being attacked.
○ Remove and burn all affected plants and do not grow parsnips, carrots, beans or plants related to the onion on the site. Some weeds may also harbour the eelworm, so weed the area regularly.

● *Neck rot* is a fungus which attacks the onion and shallot bulbs when they are still in the ground, but the symptoms are rarely seen until the bulbs are in store. The tissue around the neck of the bulb becomes soft and develops a translucent appearance, followed by the development of grey black fungal growth. Hard, black resting bodies of the fungus (sclerotia) develop around the neck. These fall into the soil and allow early infection the following year. If onions were planted these sclerotia would germinate as soon as weather conditions became favourable, and start to attack the bulb.
○ Always buy seed and sets from reputable sources. Practise crop rotation. Avoid excessive use of high nitrogen feeds, harvest bulbs carefully and

avoid injuring them, ripen them off well and ensure good storage conditions. Grow yellow or red bulb onions as these are less susceptible than white bulbs.

● *Onion fly* grubs feed on the roots and tunnel into the bulb, causing the foliage to wither and yellow and the bulbs to become totally inedible. Shallots and leeks may also be attacked. The most severe damage occurs in early to mid-summer. The larvae are up to 8 mm ($^1/_4$ in) long and are a cream colour. The pest overwinters in the soil and so crop rotation is essential (see page 14). Cultivation of the soil in winter will help ensure some natural control by birds which eat the exposed pupae.
○ Remove all affected plants and treat the soil with an insecticide such as phoxim or pirimiphos-methyl before planting.

· SPLITTING AND FORKING IN ROOT CROPS ·

Symptom	Cause	Remedy
Roots split lengthways	Irregular or erratic water supply, especially common in free-draining soils and in dry seasons, occurring when heavy rainfall or watering suddenly raise moisture levels after drought	Improve soil texture; mulch to help soil maintain moisture levels; water regularly
Roots become divided or forked	Poor soil conditions – encouraged by the presence of flints, large numbers of stones, or soil with is very heavy	Dig ground over well before sowing/planting and remove larger stones and flints
Roots become forked	Over manuring	Use manure in moderation and never use it unless it has been rotted down well

· HANDY TIP ·
Remember that onions, shallots, leeks, garlic and chives are all very closely related. If you see a disease or pest problem starting to develop on any one of these, thoroughly inspect the others.

● *Thrips* are 2–3 mm long and blackish brown or yellow. As they feed on the foliage it develops a dense silvery flecking and sometimes slight distortion. In extreme cases the foliage may die off but generally the damage looks worse than it really is. As the pests overwinter in the soil, crop rotation helps keep the problem under control.
○ Regular watering helps to keep numbers down. If necessary spray with malathion.

● *White rot* is a fungus which attacks the roots and bulb, causing poor growth and yellowing and deterioration of the foliage. Fluffy white fungal growth develops on the bulb and small black resting bodies of the fungus may also be seen.
○ Remove and burn affected plants. Do not grow onions or related plants on that site again.

Potato (Fig. 9)

● *Blackleg* is a bacterial disease that causes the deterioration of the stem base, so the foliage grows slowly and then becomes discoloured and starts to die off. Those tubers which become infected show a greyish rot. The disease is usually introduced on infected but symptomless seed potatoes.
○ Harvest potatoes very carefully as infection may occur as they are lifted. Store them well and check regularly, removing any tubers showing deterioration. Avoid potatoes known to be especially susceptible e.g. 'Desiree', 'Maris Bard' and 'Estima'.

● *Blight* first appears as inconspicuous darkish brown spots on the foliage which, in muggy weather, become covered in white fungal growth. The foliage may be reduced to a rotting mass. In warm, damp weather spores are spread rapidly and adjacent plants quickly become infected. The tubers may become infected too and develop brown sunken patches on the skin and discolouration of the flesh.

○ Clean up infected plants and remove all debris at the end of the season; carefully dig over the soil to locate any tubers. This disease may also affect tomatoes so ensure that these are also removed. Earth up new plants deeply as this cuts down on the likelihood of spores reaching the tubers. Grow resistant varieties. Space plants well to allow for better air movement between them. Apply a preventative spray with a fungicide containing copper or mancozeb according to the instructions.

● *Common scab* causes slightly raised scabby patches to develop on affected tubers, and they may also become deformed, sometimes with large cracks. The disease is especially common in gardens recently created from old grassland and when the soil is light, sandy and alkaline.

○ Peel off scabby areas and the tuber can then be eaten. Do not compost infected debris or peelings of potatoes. Incorporate plenty of organic material and water the crop frequently. Avoid liming. Grow resistant varieties.

● *Internal rust spot* symptoms are similar to those caused by spraing, but here the discoloured areas are discrete red-brown spots or small blotches. The tubers can be safely eaten as this disorder is caused by slightly inadequate growing conditions and is not infectious.

○ Keep the crop well watered. Improve soil structure by digging in bulky organic matter.

● *Potato cyst eelworm* weakens plants and they soon wither and yellow and start to collapse. Even

Fig. 9 Quite often a potato problem is only noticed when the crop is harvested or in store, but a plant kept problem free whilst growing should mean fewer problems later on.

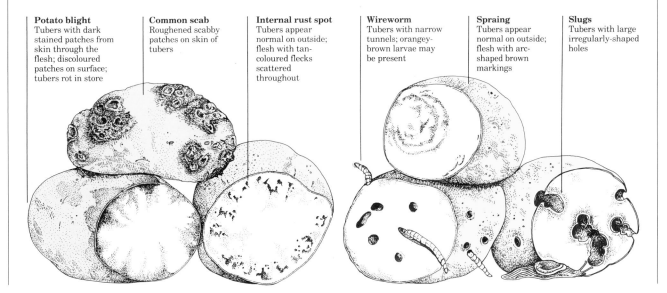

Potato blight
Tubers with dark stained patches from skin through the flesh; discoloured patches on surface; tubers rot in store

Common scab
Roughened scabby patches on skin of tubers

Internal rust spot
Tubers appear normal on outside; flesh with tan-coloured flecks scattered throughout

Wireworm
Tubers with narrow tunnels; orangey-brown larvae may be present

Spraing
Tubers appear normal on outside; flesh with arc-shaped brown markings

Slugs
Tubers with large irregularly-shaped holes

This sprouting seed tuber has several wireworms feeding on it.

more disappointing is the lack of tubers when you lift the plant! Tiny pale brown spheres may be found on the roots: these are the cysts of the eelworm and they fall into the soil and can remain viable for up to eight years. They are not easy to see, but they are worth looking for as the eelworms themselves are far too small to be seen.
○ Remove and burn affected plants, roots and all and do not grow either tomatoes or potatoes on that site for at least eight years.

● *Powdery scab* develops as scabby patches on the tuber and this may become very deformed, bearing large protuberances. Powdery scab is most troublesome in wet, poorly drained soils.
○ Do not grow potatoes on affected site for at least four , preferably longer. Remove affected tubers and do not compost debris or peelings.

● *Spraing* appears as red-brown arcs in the flesh of tubers, which may develop to the usual shape and size. This disease is caused by potato mop top virus and tobacco rattle virus, both of which are transmitted by nematodes which are especially common in light, sandy soils.
○ Infected plants cannot be cured but do not save tubers for seed and avoid future attacks by rotating crops.

● *Wart* allows the plants to grow normally, but when the tubers are lifted they are covered in large, rough warty outgrowths. Occasionally stems may show similar but smaller outgrowths.
○ This is uncommon but if you do find it in your garden you should notify the local Ministry of Agriculture, Fisheries and Food. It is more likely to cause severe distortion in wet years. It is easily

spread in soil by adhering to boots, tools and so on, and can remain viable in the soil for in excess of 30 years, even if no potatoes are grown.

● *Wireworms* are orangey-brown larvae which tunnel into the tubers, making them unappetizing and prone to rotting. The problem is usually worst on new gardens or areas of old grassland which have been recently dug over and planted up. Generally these pests are less troublesome after the land has been cultivated for a few years. Regular cultivation is therefore essential. The earlier the crop is lifted, the smaller the amount of damage to the tubers, so lift maincrop potatoes as early as possible.
○ The soil can be treated with phoxim, chlorpyrifos/diazinon or other suitable soil insecticide before the tubers are planted.

Sweet corn

● *Frit fly* larvae burrow into the young plants, causing only a few, small cobs to form. In more severe attacks, there may be no crop.
○ Reduce the risk of attack by sowing the seed towards the end of spring, or raise plants in individual pots.

● *Smut* appears as large greyish-white swellings, which burst out on the developing cobs. Male flowers and stems may occasionally be affected too. Each swelling is packed full of black fungal spores and these are released when the swelling ruptures.
Smut is most troublesome in very hot, dry summers and, although not a common problem, if it is present and the weather conditions favourable to it, many cobs may be ruined.
○ Remove affected cobs before the spores are released. Destroy all crop debris at the end of the year and use a fresh site for future crops.

HARDY VEGETABLES

Brassica (Fig. 10)

● *Cabbage white fly* cluster in their hundreds on the undersurface of the foliage and will fly up in clouds if you disturb them. Close inspection of an infested leaf should reveal pale green immature stages – 'scales' adhering closely to the undersurface of the leaf. The adults excrete a sugary honeydew which coats the plant and may become colonized by black sooty mould. These pests overwinter on brassicas and are not the same as the whitefly found in greenhouses.
○ Spray with permethrin or pirimiphos-methyl. The sticky and sooty deposits can be washed off.

● *Caterpillars,* of which the most troublesome are those of the large cabbage white butterfly, the small cabbage white butterfly and the cabbage moth. These pests rapidly eat large ragged holes in the foliage and may burrow into cabbage hearts and hide amongst the heads of broccoli and calabrese. Most damage occurs between mid-spring and the end of the summer, and seedlings may be attacked too.
○ Regularly pick off the caterpillars and squash egg clusters. Wherever possible control the infestation before these creatures burrow into the centre of the plants as once they have penetrated to any depth, control is far harder. Create a barrier with horticultural fleece to prevent the eggs from being laid.
○ Spray with an insecticide such as derris, permethrin or pyrethrum. A biological control agent, *Bacillus thuringiensis* is now available and can be sprayed onto brassicas to kill caterpillars.

● *Clubroot* stunts and discolours affected plants. Wilting is likely to occur unusually rapidly on hot days. The roots are swollen or clubbed and disintegrate into a foul-smelling mass (Fig. 11).

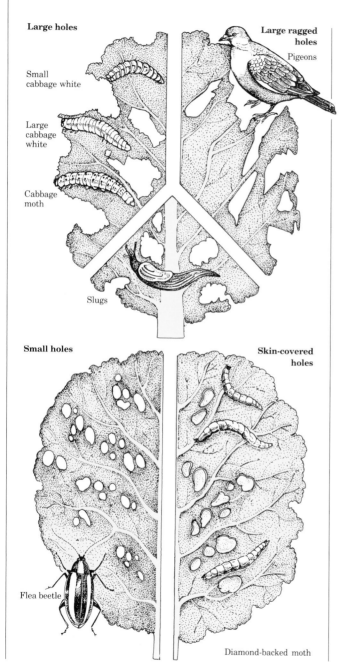

Large holes

Small
cabbage white

Large
cabbage
white

Cabbage
moth

Slugs

**Large ragged
holes**

Pigeons

Small holes

Flea beetle

**Skin-covered
holes**

Diamond-backed moth

Some closely related weeds (e.g. shepherd's purse) and ornamentals (e.g. wallflowers) may be attacked too. This disease is usually introduced in soil particles adhering to boots, wheelbarrows, tools and so on, or on infected plants. Always check purchased plants, or preferably raise your own in individual pots so that they have a well-developed root system on planting.

○ The pathogen thrives in poorly drained acid soils, so improve drainage and apply lime. Burn all affected plants and avoid moving infested soil around the garden. The pathogen may persist in the soil for over 20 years.

● *Mealy cabbage aphid* appears as dense greyish-blue colonies, clustered on the undersurface of the leaves. As they feed the leaves develop yellow patches and young foliage may become very distorted and stunted. If the buttons of Brussels sprouts or the hearts of cauliflowers are attacked, the crop may be spoiled completely. As these pests overwinter on old brassica plants, burn or deeply bury all that remains of the crop.

○ Check young plants frequently and spray with suitable insecticide (see page 94).

◄Fig. 10 Brassica leaves may become covered in holes of various shapes and sizes. It is important to discover the pest responsible as there may be different control measures.

● *Powdery mildew* appears as greyish-white powdery patches of fungal growth on the leaves and may cause them to discolour and deteriorate.
○ Pick off badly infected leaves. In severe cases, spray with thiophanate-methyl, benomyl or carbendazim.

● *Root fly* maggots eat all the fine roots and may cause extensive blue-ish discolouration and wilting, and occasionally the death of young plants. Better established brassicas may be able to tolerate a limited attack and still grow fairly well, despite some signs of distress. The injured roots may become colonized by bacteria and so rot and form an evil-smelling slime.
○ Apply a soil insecticide such as phoxim or pirimiphos-methyl when sowing and transplanting. Fit each plant with a collar of carpet underlay to prevent the eggs being laid (Fig. 12).

● *White blister* causes the leaves to appear slightly distorted and the undersurface to bear glossy white fungal spore masses, sometimes arranged in concentric circles. Occasionally cauliflower and broccoli heads may be attacked. The yield and edibility are not significantly affected.

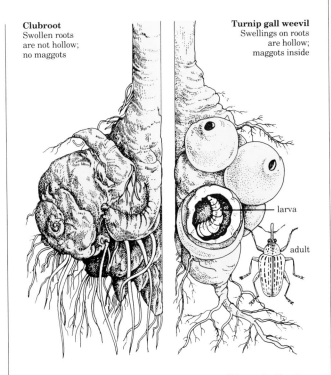

Fig. 12 Turnip gall weevil may cause swellings similar to those on a club root-infested plant. Cut the galls open to see whether they contain a weevil larva.

○ Thrives in moist conditions, so improve air circulation by keeping plants well spaced and the area weed free. Remove affected leaves.

Broad bean

● *Chocolate spot* develops as brown spots and blotches on the leaves and stems. In severe cases the foliage may die off. This disease is most common on overwintered beans in wet seasons and on plants which have been grown too soft.
○ Spray affected plants with a suitable systemic fungicide. Avoid excessive use of high-nitrogen fertilizers. Remove and burn affected plants and use a new site next year.

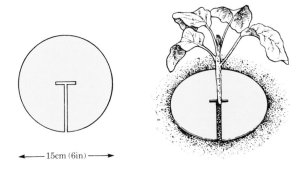

Fig. 11 For a very effective and potentially pesticide-free way of controlling cabbage root fly, fit individual brassica collars made of carpet underlay.

39

● *Pea and bean weevil* cause characteristic notching around the edge of the foliage of both broad beans and peas. The damage may look worrying but it appears to have little significant effect on the plant's growth. The adults are a greyish-brown colour and about 6 mm long, but they may be hard to find unless the plant is gently shaken and the weevils drop out.

Pea and bean weevils remove notches from the leaf edges of peas and broad beans as they feed. The plant is, however, rarely seriously affected.

○ Control the adults by squashing, and apply derris to the soil and the young plants to protect them.

Leeks

● *Rust* allows plants to grow well initially but then the outer leaves develop orange, raised 'blisters', which erupt to produce masses of bright orange spores. The affected leaves yellow and, in severe cases, may die back. Generally the eating quality of the leek is not affected as the inner parts can still be eaten.

○ Avoid excessive use of high-nitrogen fertilizers and dress the soil with sulphate of potash before planting out. Space plants well and keep the area weed free to allow good air circulation.

Parsnips

● *Canker* develops on the shoulders of the parsnip which develops discoloured patches – most commonly brown or black – which may then spread on to the shank and develop into areas of rotten tissue.

○ Apply lime if the soil pH is neutral or below. Grow the crop in a deep, well-fertilized and dug-over site, using a new area each year. Sow the seed early and thin to about 8 cm (3 in). Grow resistant varieties.

Peas (Fig. 13)

● *Pea and bean weevil* are about 6 mm long, greyish-brown and cause a characteristic notching around the edges of the leaves. The overall growth and yield of infested plants is not significantly affected. The larvae may attack the roots.

○ Collect and destroy adult weevils. Dust susceptible young plants and the surrounding soil with derris.

● *Pea moth* caterpillars feed on the developing peas inside the pod but you may only notice the extent of the problem on the pods when you harvest towards the end of the summer. The 6 mm-long caterpillars have a black head with a

▲ The bright orange spores of leek rust develop within raised pustules on the outer leaves, the inner ones are rarely affected.

▼ Parsnips attacked by canker discolour black or reddish brown around their shoulders and then the rot spreads.

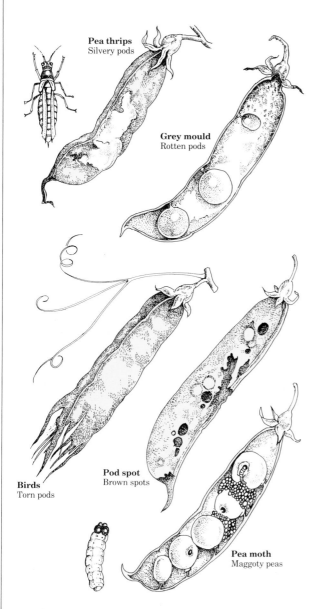

Pea thrips
Silvery pods

Grey mould
Rotten pods

Birds
Torn pods

Pod spot
Brown spots

Pea moth
Maggoty peas

Fig. 13 Pea pods can be blemished by several diseases and pests. Some, like pea thrips, only damage the outside of the pod; others, like pea moth and pod spot, cause extensive damage to the peas as well.

creamy white body. Sow quick-maturing varieties of pea to ensure that they do not flower during the moth's egg-laying period (early to late summer).
○ On peas which are in flower during the critical period, spray at dusk with an insecticide such as permethrin or fenitrothion as they come into flower.

● *Pea thrip* are tiny (2 mm), yellow (young), or black (adult), which suck sap from the pods, causing a distinct silvering and distortion. Leaves may be affected too. Hot, dry summers, in particular, encourage the pest.
○ Spray with a suitable insecticide such as permethrin, pyrethrum or malathion.

● *Pod spot* appears as dark brown sunken spots on the pods and occasionally on the leaves and stems. Individual spots may merge, so forming large discoloured patches. The fungus may then spread to the peas within the pod, and these too develop brown spots. The disease is most troublesome in wet years.
○ Burn all debris at the end of the season and use a new site. Only use seed from a reputable source and do not save suspect seed, as pod spot is seed-borne.

Salsify, Scorzonera

● *White blister* develops as shiny white spore masses on the foliage and causes distortion.
○ Space plants well. Remove and burn affected leaves. Rotate crops.

Seakale

● Black rot turns foliage yellow and leaf veins black, and a black streaking develops just under the surface. This disease is most troublesome in damp but warm seasons and on poorly drained soils.
○ Remove and burn affected plants. Improve drainage and rotate crops.

Spinach (Fig. 14)

● *Blight (CMV)* causes leaves to turn yellow and slightly distorted, often strangely narrow and with inrolled margins. Younger leaves are affected first. The virus is carried by aphids as they feed, so may spread rapidly.

❍ Remove and burn affected plants. Keep the area weed free as certain weeds may harbour this virus too. Control aphids.

● *Downy mildew* appears as yellow blotches on the upper surface of the leaf which correspond with patches of fuzzy grey or purplish-grey fungal growth on the undersurface. Badly infected leaves

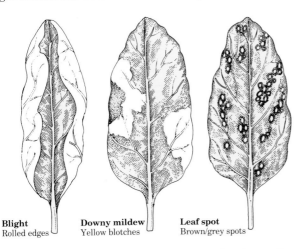

Blight
Rolled edges

Downy mildew
Yellow blotches

Leaf spot
Brown/grey spots

Fig. 14 A hand lens will come in handy for close inspection of spinach leaves as some problems, like downy mildew, may be difficult to see.

– usually the older ones – later turn quite brown and may die off completely. The fungus thrives in damp seasons and on overcrowded plants.

❍ Improve air circulation and keep the area weed free. Remove severely affected leaves and spray with mancozeb. Early control is essential if the crop is to be saved.

● *Leaf spot* appears as brown or greyish spots, often with pale centres, on the foliage and may soon become extensive, and the leaves may appear burned or scorched.

❍ Remove badly affected leaves and try to improve spacing to avoid overcrowding. Avoid excessive use of high-nitrogen feeds but apply sulphate of potash before sowing. Rotate crops.

Spinach beet

● *Leaf miner* symptoms include yellow blotch mines on the leaves, each harbouring several maggots which eat away at the inside of the leaf. Each mine later turns dry and brown and may appear slightly raised. Generally these pests have little significant effect on productivity, but young plants can suffer a severe check in growth.

❍ Pick off heavily infested leaves. Cultivate the soil in winter to expose the overwintering pupae.

Swede and turnip

● *Brown heart* appears as concentric rings of brown discolouration within affected roots. On cooking, they develop a hard, fibrous texture and are tasteless. A deficiency of boron is responsible and is especially common on very light, strongly alkaline soils.

❍ Apply borax at approximately 35 g/20 m ($1\frac{1}{4}$ oz/ $6\frac{1}{2}$ ft) before sowing. To make it easier to achieve an even distribution, mix the borax with large quantities of fine, dry, horticultural sand first.

▲ Lettuce mosaic virus (left) may cause stunting and discolouration.

▶ Globe artichokes are an attractive and delicious vegetable and look quite at home surrounded by ornamentals.

● *Cabbage root fly* causes affected plants to grow slowly. The foliage discolours and may wilt very readily because the maggots eat the fine roots and may tunnel into the swollen base too.
○ Remove affected plants. Apply a soil insecticide such as phoxim or pirimiphos-methyl at planting. Fit each plant with a 15 cm (6 in) diameter collar of carpet underlay to prevent egg laying by the adults.

● *Flea beetles* are yellow and black striped or pure black and feed on the foliage of seedlings, making numerous holes up to 2 mm in diameter. Growth may be severely checked and plants may even die. If fully grown plants are attacked, the damage is usually of little significance.
○ Ensure seedlings are well maintained so that they grow rapidly. Dust the plants and soil with derris, pyrethrum or pirimiphos-methyl.

● *Mealy cabbage aphid* are greyish-white and cluster together on the undersurface of the leaves; as they feed, they cause yellow patches to develop on the foliage. Young growth is especially prone to injury and may show severe distortion.
○ Remove all debris at the end of the season. Check plants frequently. Spray with a suitable insecticide such as permethrin.

● *Mosaic virus* distorts foliage and causes the veins to appear especially large because the area immediately adjacent to them becomes yellow ('vein clearing'). Yellow flecking or mottling may also occur. Infections occurring on young plants may be fatal and foliage of older plants usually dies back prematurely.
○ Remove affected plants even if they still appear to be fairly vigorous, as all the while they are present they allow further infections to occur. Spray against aphids as these pests transmit the virus as they feed.

● *Soft rot* will destroy swedes and turnips quite rapidly either in the ground or in store, especially if conditions are rather damp. Affected crops may have a very unpleasant smell. Infection usually occurs via the leaf stalk bases or through a root or crown injury.
○ Avoid injury to any part of the plant at all stages of development. Improve drainage and avoid excessive use of manure.

● *Turnip gall weevil* develops as rounded swellings on the roots and stem bases, outwardly similar to clubroot but when cut open each is seen to be hollow (Fig. 11, page 39). Each gall contains a weevil grub which later leaves, via a small circular hole, to pupate in the soil. Despite the appearance of these galls, with the exception of turnips, growth is not usually significantly affected.
○ Remove all crop debris.

PERENNIAL VEGETABLES

Globe artichoke

● *Petal blight* appears as pale brown spots on the young, developing heads and may merge to form large patches (Fig.15). In extreme cases the whole head may rot, leaving you with no crop at all! This disease is fairly rare but, if it does occur and damp conditions are prevalent, it will rapidly cause a great deal of damage. The same fungus attacks chrysanthemums and dahlias and may spread from one host to another.

○ Cut off and destroy infected heads. Spray plants with mancozeb.

● *Root aphids* cluster around the roots, which are often in a white waxy powder. As they feed on the sap they weaken the plant and may disrupt transport by the roots. Infested plants therefore start to grow slowly, may be discoloured and wilt. Infested plants may survive and crop but those which show severe symptoms are best removed immediately.

○ Drench plant roots with malathion.

Fig. 15 Petal blight on globe artichoke is most likely to occur in damp seasons and may be locally common but is rarely widespread. Light brown spots appear and the head soon rots.

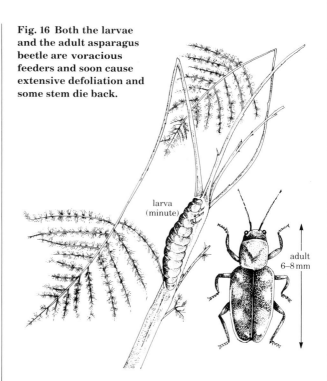

Fig. 16 Both the larvae and the adult asparagus beetle are voracious feeders and soon cause extensive defoliation and some stem die back.

larva (minute)

adult 6–8 mm

Asparagus

● *Asparagus beetle* causes extensive damage to the foliage and stems, and in extreme cases causes the death of all the top growth. The adults are 6–8 mm long and have a red and black body with a pattern of yellow squares on it and a black head; they may cause extensive defoliation (Fig. 16). There may be several generations a year and so feeding injury may be seen from late spring until the end of summer. The larvae are a greyish-cream colour and may also do a great deal of damage. Even if the plant is not killed outright, if the attack is extensive the vigour of the plant and its cropping will be noticeably reduced.

○ Pick off adults and larvae regularly. Spray with an insecticide containing permethrin. Clean up all debris at the end of the season.

● *Fusarium* causes plants to yellow and die back, but inspection of both the top growth and the root and crown area may reveal no obvious signs of the cause of deterioration. Fusarium is a microscopic soil-borne fungus which kills off the roots and may cause some staining of the inside of infected roots.
○ Affected or suspect plants should be removed and burned and a new site used.

● *Violet root rot* is a soil-borne fungus which attacks and kills the roots and crowns, covering them with dark violet fungal strands. The foliage yellows and dies back because the roots can no longer function adequately. The fungus grows through the soil, attacking other asparagus plants and also carrots, beetroot and parsnips. If the infection is caught early it may be possible to isolate the infested area by removing all infected or suspect plants and sinking barriers of heavy-duty polythene to a depth of 30 cm (12 in). Generally, however, beds which have shown infection are best discarded and not used for growing susceptible crops.
○ Control weeds in the area, such as dandelion and docks as these may also harbour the infection.

Rhubarb

● *Crown rot* is a soil-borne bacterial disease which causes a slow deterioration of the crown and dieback, until the sticks remaining are very undersized and spindly. The bacteria are likely to be especially troublesome in heavy, wet soils: they usually cause damage via a point of injury, but soon attack the terminal bud and also cause internal rotting just below the crown which causes a cavity to develop.
○ Remove infected plants together with the crown and roots. Choose a fresh site for any new crowns and try to improve the soil texture before planting.

GREENHOUSE VEGETABLES

Aubergines

● *Verticillium wilt* is a soil-borne fungal infection which can be especially troublesome on young plants – as a result of the roots being attacked, the older or lower leaves soon show signs of yellowing. Necrotic brown patches later develop on the leaves and the plant may show signs of wilting. If the stem is cut open there may be signs of a brown discolouration running the length of the stem.
○ There is no cure so affected plants should be removed and burned. If the plants were grown in the greenhouse borders, change the soil before the area is re-used.

Peppers

● *Blossom end rot* causes the flower end of the developing fruit to fail to colour up normally, and it becomes tough and leathery and may shrink inwards. On ripe peppers the area is usually dark brown or black (Fig. 17). This disorder is due to a deficiency of calcium within the developing fruits. It is encouraged by a heavy crop, acidic growing media, and by erratic or inadequate watering. Plants in growing bags or pots are especially prone. During conditions of low moisture around the roots, even if there is plenty of calcium in the soil or compost, the plant is not able to take it up. Affected fruits are safe to eat.
○ Keep plants well fed and watered and remove ripe fruits as soon as possible.

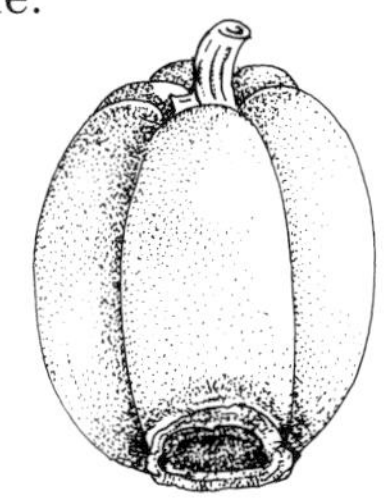

Fig. 17 Blossom end rot causes distinctive sunken and blackened leathery patches on the base of tomato and pepper fruits.

47

• 4 •
Herb Clinic

There is nothing like the extra flavour and excitement which you can so easily add to cooking, just by using a few select herbs. Where would a curry dish be without the addition of chopped coriander leaves, spaghetti bolognaise without a bay leaf or two lurking in its depths, sage and onion stuffing without the sage? Of course it is not just our cooking which is so enhanced by herbs, there is the delightful summertime drink to be enjoyed with mint. Herbs are often fairly inconspicuous, but we would certainly notice it if they were not around!

Even if you only have a tiny garden, or indeed just a window box, you should try growing some of your favourites. Most herbs are readily available as seeds or, for a more instant effect why not treat yourself to a few of the small pots which are stocked by many garden centres. Just one word of warning: if you really have got a restricted space, do check to see the potential sizes of the plants you select, because a few, like bay and rosemary can grow to become large shrubs or, in the case of the bay, a tree.

If you can grow your herbs close to the house you will benefit in two ways: first there will be some protection provided by the house and, when you need the herbs in a hurry (or on a dark, wet night) you will not have to go traipsing to the bottom of the garden… and, of course, if you plant up a window box you will probably not even have to venture outside at all!

Generally, herbs are fairly trouble free but they do occasionally suffer attacks by pests or diseases. The problem is that in most cases we eat the foliage and so if this becomes infested with a disfiguring problem, it is particularly off-putting. Again, because the foliage is usually consumed or cooked in with the food, you may feel reluctant to rely on chemical sprays, so prevention may need to be more heavily relied upon. In some cases the infested area or the pest itself can simply be removed, leaving perfectly edible material behind; but there is no doubt that you may well need to use a spray on some problems, in which case you should remember that when any chemical is used on a plant you are going to use as food or in cooking, you *must* observe the harvest interval (see page 23).

Bay

● *Bay sucker* The edges of the leaves fold over and become thickened and yellow during the summer, the young suckers develop within this part of the leaf. The adults feed on the foliage and this may cause some distortion and discolouration too.
○ Pick off affected leaves as they are seen. There may be more than one generation a year, so check

▶ **A window box full of herbs provides an easily accessible source of perfectly fresh herbs for use in the kitchen. Even if you have no garden you could still have a mini-herb garden in your window box.**

48

the plant regularly. Spray with dimethoate twice during late spring. Clean up all debris near the bay tree at the end of the season as this may help somewhat to remove some of the overwintering adult suckers.

● *Soft scale* is usually first noticed by the sticky patches on leaves, followed by black sooty growths. The pests themselves are less obvious and are usually found on the lower surfaces of the leaves, mainly clustered along the veins, or sometimes on the stems. The scales are waxy and pale yellowy brown, oval and anything up to 4 mm long. The scales suck the bay's sap and this has such a high sugar content that they cannot digest it all; so their excreta, commonly known as honeydew, is extremely sticky. As it falls onto the leaves below, it therefore forms a sticky layer and this later becomes colonized by sooty mould fungi. Unless it forms a very dense layer, this fungus is perfectly harmless and just feeds on the honeydew.

○ Spray the lower surfaces of the foliage with malathion or pirimiphos-methyl every 14 days. When the scales have been killed you can clean up the sooty mould with a sponge and soapy water.

Mint

● *Rust* affects the young growth as it emerges in the late spring, causing the stems to become distorted and strangely swollen, the swellings being covered in orange fungal pustules. Occasionally stems are killed but they usually continue to grow and become increasingly distorted. The leaves become infected and fall prematurely.

○ Remove affected stems immediately to decrease spread of the disease. A new mint bed can be created on a new site using cuttings from healthy plants.

Parsley

● *Aphids and viruses* are a joint problem in that aphids may infest parsley and cause a certain degree of stunting and poor growth but they then frequently transmit virus diseases as they feed. The most troublesome of these are carrot red leaf and carrot motley dwarf viruses, which together cause carrot motley dwarf disease. Affected plants are very stunted and may be distorted, and the foliage develops a distinct yellow and later red colouration. The individual leaflets become narrowed and distorted. Do not confuse these symptoms with those of magnesium deficiency, where the plant only shows the symptoms of discolouration and need not be destroyed.

○ Remove and burn the plants as they will die gradually and cannot be cured. Spray against aphids with heptenophos/permethrin or dimethoate, or a suitable fatty acid spray.

· OTHER COMMON PROBLEMS ON HERBS ·		
Problem	**Description**	**Control**
Aphid	Vary in colour but are most commonly shades of green, pale brown; found in clusters especially on soft young growth	Heptenophos/ permethrin or dimethoate, or a suitable fatty acid spray
Downy mildew	Fuzzy white or purplish-white patches on the under-surface of leaves, corresponding with yellow blotches	Pick off affected areas; spray with mancozeb
Leafhoppers	White flecks on the foliage, often so dense that the leaf may appear almost white in patches	Spray with heptenophos/ permethrin, dimethoate
Powdery mildew	A white powdery fungal layer appears, mainly on the upper surfaces of leaves; distortion and deterioration may follow	Remove affected areas; spray with a fungicide e.g. carbendazim, benomyl

· 5 ·
Fruit Clinic

Growing your own fruit enables you to choose from favourites without being restricted to the small range available in the shops. Many of the older, less commercially viable varieties may have a better taste and texture.

Although you will almost always get a good or at least reasonable crop, there is always the risk that it will be beset by a wide range of pests, diseases and disorders. You may need to spray against certain pests or diseases before you actually see symptoms – this preventative spraying has to be timed accurately, but does prove extremely effective. Not all pesticides are suitable for use on edible crops, so check that the product carries a label recommendation for use on your chosen crops. The label will also indicate the minimum period which must elapse between spraying and eating (the so-called 'harvest interval').

The best way to minimize the damage done by pests and diseases is often to spray regularly and frequently. This is not to say you should choose or use the chemicals indiscriminately, but you can control most of the common problems using a fairly restricted range of products. The key to success is to use a fruit-spraying programme which is based around the stage of development that the fruit is at – spraying programmes are most frequently used on tree fruits, and to help you a fruit spraying programme is included on page 91.

This will not appeal to everyone, as it does go against the current trend towards organic gardening. If you would prefer to restrict, or indeed avoid spraying, you can spray where necessary or concentrate on the cultural methods suggested.

Whenever using chemicals remember to follow the instructions on the pack carefully with regard to timing, application rate, harvest interval etc.

● *Wound paints.* Years ago the use of a wound paint on all pruning wounds was recommended. However, research has shown that these treatments are in fact either of no benefit or sometimes even detrimental, as they may act as barriers which protect the fungal infection rather than the tree! Nowadays they are recommended only for trees which are susceptible to 'fresh wound parasites', notably fruit trees and especially *Prunus* spp., which are readily attacked by silver leaf, and also apples and pears which are attacked by fungal canker. Wounds on these should be painted immediately.

Apple (Fig. 18)

● *Bitter pit* is a deficiency which causes brown flecks to develop within the flesh. Sometimes the skin shows brown slightly sunken spots too. The apple may develop an unpleasant, bitter taste. The symptoms may appear while the fruits are on the

◄ The creamy white fungal pustules of brown rot are full of spores, so dispose of infected fruits promptly.

tree, but the condition usually worsens in stored fruits. Bitter pit is due to a calcium deficiency within the fruit but there may be plenty of calcium in the soil. Dry soil restricts the tree's ability to take up calcium even if it is present in abundance. Excess potash may have a similar effect. Vigorous trees and those producing heavy crops of large fruits are most likely to be affected.

○ Water thoroughly and regularly. Mulch well. Summer prune to reduce vigour. Spray developing fruits with calcium nitrate from mid-summer onwards.

● *Blossom wilt* appears shortly after flowering, when the blossoms become brown, wither and die, followed by adjacent bunches of leaves and sometimes spurs. Inspection with a hand lens reveals masses of creamy-buff-coloured pustules.

○ Cut out affected areas. Spray with carbendazim or benomyl as blossoming begins.

● *Brown rot* causes rapid devastation and may develop on fruits on the tree or in store. The fungus is only capable of damaging fruits which have already been injured, for example from attack by codling moth, birds, wasps, apple scab. Affected fruit turn soft and brown and concentric rings of creamy white pustules break out all over the surface.
○ Remove affected fruits. Never leave fallen fruit beneath a tree. Avoid injury to the fruits by keeping other pests and diseases at bay. Water frequently to prevent fruit crack. Store only perfect fruits and inspect regularly.

● *Canker* appears as discoloured, sunken elliptical patches on woody stems, large branches, or the trunk of the tree. Loose, flakey concentric rings of bark then develop on these areas. The canker increases in size and may girdle the stem/branch. Foliage above the canker grows poorly and dies, together with the stem.
○ Prune out affected areas or cut out cankers on larger branches. Apply a wound paint. Spray with a copper fungicide.

● *Capsid bugs* are pale green and 5–6 mm ($1/_8$ in) long. From mid-spring they suck the sap of the young foliage and then the fruitlets; their saliva causes small, hard protuberances or occasionally scabby patches to form. The foliage develops numerous tiny holes. It is best to peel damaged areas before eating.
○ Spray with heptenophos or pirimiphos-methyl.

● *Codling moths* lay their eggs in early summer and when they have hatched the caterpillars tunnel into the fruit, feeding as they go and creating a path

▲ **Apple-scab infected fruits often crack, so allowing other fungi to attack.**

▶ **Young shoots may harbour apple-scab infection, so ensure that they are pruned out.**

full with frass. They feed until late summer and then hide away under flakes of loose bark on the trunk. The apple ripens prematurely and is left with a brownish exit hole; it may still be edible if you are prepared to cut out the tunnelled area.

○ Spray trees with fenitrothion, pirimiphos-methyl or permethrin (see page 94). Encourage birds in the garden as these will eat the caterpillars. During mid-summer, scrape off loose bark and wrap hessian around the trunk to provide an 'overwintering site' which can then be removed and burned, together with the caterpillars, in late autumn. Use pheromone traps from late spring to monitor the males and allow you to spray at the best possible time.

● *Fruit tree red spider mites* suck the sap on the lower surface of the leaves, causing mottling and discolouration. They are particularly troublesome in hot, dry seasons and foliage may fall early.

○ Spray with malathion.

● *Papery bark* develops if growing conditions are not ideal, especially if the soil is heavy, compacted or waterlogged, when the bark may start to peel away in pale brown, paper-thin sheets. Girdling may occur, resulting in dieback.

○ Remove affected areas and improve growing conditions. Pay particular attention to improving drainage.

● *Powdery mildew* develops as a dense white powdery fungal growth which coats the foliage. New growth on shoot tips may be badly distorted. In extreme cases the leaves die and they fall prematurely.

○ Prune out severely infected growth. Clear up fallen leaves. Spray with carbendazim or benomyl.

● *Sawfly* causes apples which have been attacked to fall before they are mature. At a later stage a brown narrow band-shaped scar is formed when the

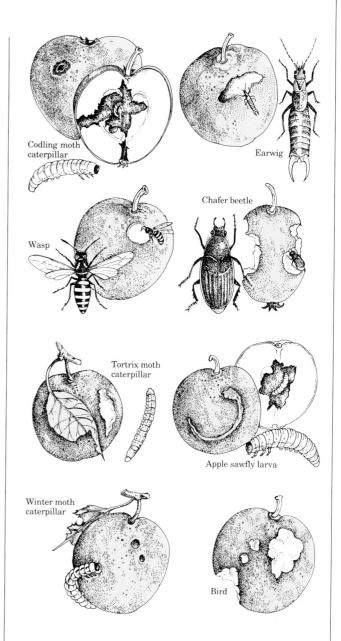

Codling moth caterpillar

Earwig

Chafer beetle

Wasp

Tortrix moth caterpillar

Apple sawfly larva

Winter moth caterpillar

Bird

Fig. 18 Holes in the surface of apples may be caused by a variety of pests.

· HANDY TIP ·

If shoot tips are deformed and damaged by diseases don't wait until the usual pruning time to remove them, do it immediately – the chances are that the growth will never mature anyway and all the while it provides a source of infection.

sawfly maggot (creamy-white in colour and up to 15 mm ($\frac{1}{2}$ in) long) tunnels just beneath the skin. Further damage is caused when it tunnels through the flesh towards the core. The fruits become distorted.

○ Spray trees with fenitrothion, HCH, pyrethrum or permethrin. Collect up and burn the fallen fruits.

● *Scab* is a fungus that attacks the foliage and fruits, causing grey-brown or black scabby patches. The leaves may become blistered and distorted. The even swelling of the fruit may be restricted by the patches of fungal growth, so they may be small, distorted and cracked. Scabby areas may appear on the shoots.

○ Prune out infection on shoots. Rake up and burn fallen leaves. Spray with carbendazim, benomyl or mancozeb.

Apricot

● *Bacterial canker* appears as flattened patches on the stems and exudes an amber-coloured gum. Leaves on all parts of the tree may show 'shot hole' symptoms where bacteria kill off small areas, causing them to go brown and drop out, leaving holes.

○ Prune out cankered branches. Spray with a copper fungicide.

● *Blossom wilt* causes newly-opened blossoms to wither and brown and remain on the tree. Adjacent bunches of leaves then deteriorate and the shoot may die back. Close inspection reveals creamy-buff pustules on the affected areas.

○ Cut out infection, spray with benomyl or carbendazim.

Cherry

● *Blackfly* are pests which may be found clustered under the leaves, causing extensive distortion and some yellowing. In early summer they fly to bedstraws, their summer hosts, but the leaves still remain curled.

○ Apply tar oil winter wash to kill overwintering eggs. In spring spray with heptenophos/permethrin or pirimicarb. Control bedstraws.

● *Blossom wilt* withers and browns new blossoms which then remain on the tree. Adjacent bunches of leaves deteriorate and the shoot dies back. Close inspection with a hand lens reveals creamy-buff fungal pustules.

○ Cut out infection and spray with benomyl or carbendazim.

● *Silver leaf* attacks isolated branches and ultimately the whole tree, indicated by a silvering of the foliage. The following year the affected branches start to deteriorate and die rapidly. It may take several years for the tree to die. Fungal fruiting bodies develop on dead wood and larger affected limbs bear a central brownish stain. The spores enter any fresh wounds e.g. pruning cuts and frost cracks, and produce toxins which cause the leaf symptoms. The tree is usually killed but it is worth trying to save it.

○ Prune out infected limbs to at least 15 cm (6 in) past the stain in the wood. Only prune susceptible trees during summer as during these months infection is less likely to occur. Always use a wound paint as soon as the cut has been made. Avoid unnecessary pruning.

● *Tan bark* is a disorder that causes tiny masses of tan-coloured powder (made up of dead plant cells) to burst out from around the lenticels (breathing pores) on the bark of one-year-old shoots, or on the trunk. This is not infectious. The vigour of the tree is rarely affected, but it does suggest that the soil is rather waterlogged.

○ Improve drainage.

Currant – black, red, white

● *American gooseberry mildew* has recently started to attack blackcurrants, covering the foliage and sometimes the stems with white powdery spores. The young leaves are most severely affected and become distorted, stunted, and may wither and die.

○ Prune out affected shoots – this will not only remove the infected area, but also help to keep the bush open and so allow good air circulation which will deter infection. Spray with a copper-based fungicide, bupirimate with triforine or carbendazim. Keep gooseberries in the area clear of infection too.

● *Big bud and reversion* are caused by mites that live concealed within the buds of blackcurrants, causing them to swell and become rounded. The infested buds may die or, if leaves are formed, they are an abnormal shape. The mites are responsible for spreading reversion, a virus-like disease which causes the development of magenta-coloured flower buds. When this occurs, the foliage on the basal shoots becomes narrowed and the main lobe on each leaf has fewer than five pairs of veins.

○ Early attacks of big bud may occasionally be controlled by regular removal of the infected buds as soon as they are seen, but it usually proves necessary to remove and burn affected bushes.

● *Capsid bugs* cause tiny holes on the young leaves. As the foliage expands, the damaged areas

◄ The swollen bud is infested with big bud mite; the healthy one (left) is smaller and more pointed.

▲ Peach leaf curl causes the leaves to pucker and discolour and to fall early.

57

are stretched, giving a tattered appearance to the plant. Foliage is distorted. The pale green bug is up to 6 mm ($1/_4$ in) long and sucks the sap; as it does so, toxins present in its saliva kill off tiny spots on the leaves which later form holes (Fig. 19).

○ Spray with heptenophos/permethrin or dimethoate. Clear up garden debris to reduce overwintering sites.

● *Leaf spot* appears as tiny dark brown or grey spots on affected leaves, which may merge. Leaf fall is premature and so the plant may be completely bare by mid-summer and can be weakened.

○ Spray with mancozeb, carbendazim or benomyl. Rake up and burn affected leaves. Keep the bush well fed and watered to encourage new growth, but avoid excessive use of high-nitrogen fertilizers.

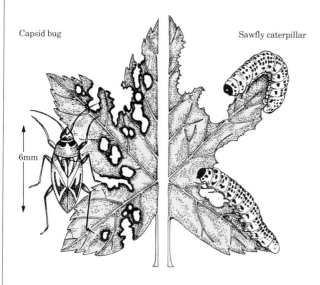

Capsid bug

Sawfly caterpillar

6mm

Fig. 19 Currents and gooseberries can be attacked by capsid bugs and sawfly caterpillars, both of which have distinctive eating habits. Capsid bugs may be hard to find but the tattered holes in the somewhat distorted foliage are very characteristic. Sawfly caterpillars usually feed on the leaf blades, with the leaf veins left as skeletal remains.

Gooseberry

● *American gooseberry mildew* develops on young leaves which become covered in a dense white layer of fungal spores. They are distorted and discoloured, and usually wither and die. Stems may be attacked too. Infected berries are covered in white fungal growth which later turns pale brown. The berries may remain small and crack. Fruits which develop to their full size are edible provided the fungal layer is rubbed off – but on cooking the berries turn brown.

○ Prune out affected shoots and leaves. Spray with a copper fungicide, triforine/bupirimate or carbendazim. Prune to keep the bush open and allow good air circulation.

● *Leaf spot* appears as tiny dark brown or grey spots which may merge covering the leaves. Defoliation occurs rapidly and prematurely, and causes loss of vigour.

○ Rake up and destroy affected leaves. Spray with mancozeb, carbendazim or benomyl. Keep the bush well fed and watered to encourage new growth, but avoid excessive use of high-nitrogen fertilizers.

● *Sawfly* caterpillars can rapidly cause very extensive damage as they eat away the leaf on gooseberries (and sometimes red and white currants), starting low down at the centre of the bush and leaving only the leaf veins. There are usually several caterpillars on the plant at any one time, each a pale green colour with many black spots (Fig. 19). Although they do not attack the fruits, the crop will decrease if the pest is not controlled.

○ Pick off and destroy caterpillars. Spray with malathion, heptenophos/permethrin.

Melon

● *Mosaic virus* causes leaves to reduce in size, distort and become covered in yellow mosaic patterns. The plant's growth is retarded or halted and it may not even flower.

○ Remove and burn affected plants. There is no cure. The main means by which it is spread is by handling (always handle infected or suspicious plants last), and by aphids as they feed (control aphids). Remove other affected plants (weeds, ornamentals, or edible crops), as they may harbour the virus.

● *Powdery mildew* appears as a dense white layer of fungal spores which cause the foliage to wither, brown and die.

○ Improve air circulation and keep the plant well watered. Pick off affected leaves. Spray with benomyl or carbendazim.

● *Red spider mite* damage appears on foliage as a fine yellowish-white mottling. The leaves dry and turn brown before falling, or occasionally remain on the plant. Webbing may be seen, especially with heavier infestations, and the plant may collapse. The sap-feeding culprits are less than 1 mm in length and are a greeny-yellow colour with two dark spots. They only turn red in the autumn.

○ Red spider mite reproduce very rapidly and may be resistant to most insecticides, but they can be dusted with malathion or sprayed with pirimiphos-methyl or malathion. Ensure high humidity as they prefer dry conditions; spray foliage with water. Consider using the predatory mite *Phytoseiulus persimilis* (see page 83).

Peach and nectarine

● *Peach leaf curl* causes the leaves to become distorted and swollen, soon becoming red or purple. Later a white film of fungal spores develops over the leaf. Leaves fall early and the tree may put on a second flush of foliage. This is rarely affected but the tree may be badly weakened.

○ Pick off affected leaves as soon as possible. The spores lodge themselves in crevices in the bark and in bud scales, so spray before the leaves first break – twice during mid-winter, with a two-week gap between. Use a copper-based fungicide. Erect a shelter to prevent spores landing and causing infection.

● *Powdery mildew* appears as a dense white layer of fungal spores on foliage, particularly the new growth. Affected leaves are stunted and distorted, unless infection occurs late in the season. Shoots may be attacked. Occasionally the fruits show similar white fungal patches.

○ Pick off affected leaves. Spray with carbendazim, bupirimate/triforine. Keep the tree well watered, but avoid wetting the foliage.

● *Red spider mite* damage covers foliage in a dense white, fine mottling which then dries up, turns brown and falls or remains on the tree. Webbing may be seen, especially if the infestation is heavy. They are a greenish-yellow colour and only become red in the autumn.

○ Red spider mite reproduce rapidly and are resistant to most of the available insecticides, but try dusting with malathion or spraying with pirimiphos-methyl or malathion. Keep humidity high and mist the foliage as they prefer dry conditions. On peaches growing in greenhouses, consider using the predatory mite *Phytoseiulus persimilis* (see page 83).

Raspberry beetles lay their eggs on flowers of raspberries, loganberries and blackberries. The larvae then feed on the ripening fruit.

● *Split stone* occurs after the peach develops, causing the fruit to split at the stalk end and allow earwigs to hide within! Ripening may not be completed before the fruit rots.
○ This physiological disorder occurs when growing conditions are unsuitable, such as caused by an irregular supply of moisture at the roots (water well and regularly, and apply a mulch), poor pollination (pollinate by hand and syringe the flowers with water), insufficient lime in the soil (add lime to bring the soil to a pH of 6.8–7.0) or inadequate feeding.

Pear

● *Blossom wilt* browns and withers newly opened blossom. Adjacent bunches of leaves and the spur then die back. Affected flowers remain on the tree. Close inspection with a hand lens reveals creamy-buff fungal pustules.
○ Prune out affected areas. Spray with carbendazim or benomyl.

● *Caterpillars* eat holes in the foliage, giving the leaf a ragged appearance. It is unlikely that the tree will be significantly affected.
○ Pick off pests and, if necessary, spray with heptenophos/permethrin or fenitrothion.

● *Fireblight* enters through the flowers and causes them to die; this is followed by death of the spur and its leaves, and the damage may spread into larger branches or into the main trunk. The dead foliage remains on the tree. In spring and autumn small cankers may be seen on affected branches and these produce droplets of bacteria in the spring which can cause new infections. If the bark is pared away, the foxy-brown tissue beneath can be seen.
○ Spread of fireblight may be prevented if prompt action is taken, but affected areas will have to be removed to a point at least 60 cm (2 ft) past the discolouration. This may render the tree unacceptable and it may be best to have it felled and burned. The interests of other fruit growers or commercial orchards in the vicinity should be considered.

● *Leaf blister* or mite appears as rows of pale green raised spots which turn dark pink and then brown. You need a hand lens to see the tiny mites, which feed within the raised spots (Fig. 20).
○ If caught early, a minor infestation may be controlled if all affected leaves are removed. Fruiting is rarely badly affected.

● *Pear midge* prevents fruitlets from swelling, and causes them to blacken and fall. The maggots of this midge are orangey-white and about 2 mm in length; they feed within the fruitlet, causing it to rot. In severe cases there may be no useful crop!
○ The maggots leave the fruitlets and pupate in the soil, so collect and burn all fallen fruitlets to reduce the population next year. Spray with heptenophos/permethrin, fenitrothion or pirimiphos-methyl.

A small strawberry cage can be constructed quickly and simply using timber and chicken wire.

● *Scab* develops as blackish-green scabby patches on the leaves and causes slight blistering. Leaves fall early. Infected fruits develop similar scabby patches but they may also be quite corky in texture. The scabs are restricted to the skin, and the flesh beneath should be edible unless secondary infection by other organisms has occurred. In severe cases the fruit may never reach full size, or may be distorted and cracked.

○ The fungus may overwinter as scabby patches on the stems, so prune these out. Rake up and burn affected leaves. Spray with carbendazim, benomyl or mancozeb.

● *Stoney pit virus* causes a knobbly appearance on fruits, which are noticeably pitted. They are unpleasant to eat as they are full of hard, dead stone cells. Usually the tree is affected branch by branch.

○ Remove affected trees.

Plum

● *Bacterial canker* causes flattened patches to develop on the stems and branches, which exude an amber-coloured gum, gradually destroying the foliage. Leaves may show 'shot hole' symptoms (see facing page).
○ Prune out cankered branches. Spray with a copper fungicide.

● *Blossom wilt* browns and withers newly opened blossom, which remain on the tree. Adjacent bunches of leaves deteriorate and the spur may die back. Close inspection reveals creamy-buff pustules.
○ Cut out infection. Spray with carbendazim or benomyl.

● *False silver leaf* symptoms may be caused by unsuitable growing conditions, inadequate feeding or irregular water availability. In contrast with silver leaf disease, the whole of the tree is affected, not just isolated limbs, and there is no stain in the wood.
○ Improve feeding regime and ensure adequate water is supplied.

● *Leaf curling aphids* feed clustered together under the leaves, especially new growth. The foliage curls or rolls tightly and becomes very puckered and sometimes discoloured. They may also produce sticky honeydew or excreta. In early or mid-summer they fly to infest a range of herbaceous plants which act as their summer hosts. Unless the leaves are inspected early in the season, the aphids themselves may no longer be in evidence, but the damage caused, together with cast skins, will give the culprit away!
○ Use a tar oil winter wash to kill overwintering eggs. In spring spray with heptenophos/permethrin or pirimicarb. Control aphids on herbaceous plants too.

● *Rust* appears as bright yellow-orange spore masses on the underside of the leaves, each corresponding with a yellow spot on the upper surface. These then turn into dark brown spore masses. Rust generally develops towards the end of the summer or in early autumn as the weather gets cooler and damper and so, although it causes premature leaf fall, it rarely affects the tree's overall vigour.
○ Rake up and burn affected leaves. Check anemones for signs of rust, as they are the alternate host for this fungus.

● *Sawfly* larva is a creamy colour and up to 15 mm ($\frac{1}{2}$ in) long. It tunnels into the fruit, causing it to drop prematurely. Each grub may attack several young plums and towards the end of the summer it hibernates in the soil. Fruits which have been attacked have a small hole on the skin, surrounded by brown excreta. Severe infestations can cause a great reduction in crop.
○ Spray with HCH, heptenophos/permethrin or fenitrothion.

Shot hole   Leaf blister mite

Fig. 20 Initial appearances can be deceptive: the holes on plum leaves caused by the disease shot hole can be easily mistaken for a pest symptom; whilst small raised spots on pear leaves, which might seem to indicate disease, are in fact caused by leaf blister mite.

● *Shot hole* makes the leaves look as if they have suffered insect attack and are covered in holes (Fig. 20). In fact the damage occurs when bacteria land on the leaves and kill small areas of leaf tissue. Brown spots develop and later fall away, leaving holes.

○ Check for bacterial canker (see page 62).

● *Silver leaf* causes silvering of isolated branches and ultimately the whole tree. The following year the affected branches show signs of deterioration and die rapidly. It takes several years for the tree to be killed. Fungal fruiting bodies develop on dead wood and affected larger limbs bear a central brownish stain. The spores enter any fresh wounds e.g. pruning cuts and frost cracks, and produce toxins which cause the leaf symptoms. The tree is usually killed but it may be worth trying to save it.

○ Prune out infected limbs to at least 15 cm (6 in) past the stain in the wood. Only prune susceptible trees during summer as during these months infection is less likely to occur. Apply wound paint as soon as the cut has been made. Avoid unnecessary pruning.

Quince

● *Quince leaf blight* causes small, angular, irregularly shaped spots to develop on leaves; they are dark red, but quickly turn dark grey. The spots may coalesce and the whole leaf yellows and falls prematurely. Occasionally fruit may develop similar spots and the disease can also cause shoot-tip dieback.

○ Rake up and burn affected leaves and prune out infected shoots.

Raspberry, blackberry, loganberry

● *Cane blight* causes dark purple-brown patches to develop towards the base of the canes, and makes leaves wilt. The canes become rather brittle and are therefore easily broken. The fungus enters via wounds, such as those caused by frost crack or cane midge attack.

○ Remove and burn affected canes, cutting to below ground level. Spray with Bordeaux mixture. Control cane midge by spraying with fenitrothion.

· COMMON VIRUSES OF SOFT FRUIT ·		
Virus	**Symptoms**	**Spread by**
● RASPBERRY		
Arabis mosaic	Small, distorted leaves with yellow flecks	Eelworms
Raspberry mosaic	Yellow blotching or mosaic patterns on the foliage, often only between the veins; leaves curled and puckered; plants are stunted and gradually decline	Aphids
Stunt	Numerous thin, spindly and stunted shoots form the stool; few flowers and these may be distorted; plants soon die	Leafhoppers
Yellow blotch	Fruiting canes die back, young canes are stunted and the lower leaves blotched	Aphids
● STRAWBERRY		
Arabis mosaic	Mottling and distortion of the crinkled foliage; sometimes with bright yellow blotches or reddish spots; symptoms most obvious in spring	Eelworms
Crinkle	Yellow and sometimes reddish spots on small leaves, followed by crinkling and puckering	Aphids
Little leaf	Yellow edges on new foliage, with some leaf curling; short stems, giving a dwarf effect; rapid deterioration	Aphids

Grape powdery mildew can attack the foliage and infected berries are small and cracked.

● *Crown gall* develops as canes rupture along their length to produce rough-surfaced or knobbly galls. The bacteria responsible enter via wounds and are often present in the soil. Secondary infections may enter the cane as a result of the rupturing.

○ Cut out affected canes. If the problem is extensive, remove the whole plant and replant on a new, better drained site.

● *Raspberry beetles* have whitey-brown-coloured larvae (6 mm or $1/4$ in long), which feed on the outside of the fruits and tunnel towards the centre – leaving dry brown patches at the stalk end and the larva feeding actively within. They later leave the fruit and pupate in the soil.

○ Spray with fenitrothion, heptenophos/permethrin or malathion, or dust with derris.

• *Spur blight* develops as dark purple blotches around the nodes of canes. The infection usually occurs early in the summer but the symptoms are not obvious until late summer. Later the patches become silvery and covered in tiny black pin-prick-sized spots (the fruiting bodies of the fungus) on the affected areas. The buds are either killed or else they produce weak and short-lived shoots.
○ Avoid overcrowded canes developing as these encourage disease development. Cut out affected canes. Spray young canes with carbendazim or benomyl.

• *Virus diseases* frequently attack raspberries. A variety of symptoms may be produced – leaf mosaic patterns, distortion, poor growth and fruiting – but in all cases affected plants should be removed. No cure is yet available and unfortunately the viruses are also easily spread.
○ Control aphids as these may act as vectors. Plant new canes on a fresh site.

Strawberry

• *Eelworm* cause plants to stay small, become distorted and have small leaves. The eelworm are not visible to the naked eye.
○ Dig up and burn affected plants.

• *Leaf spot* covers older leaves in small purple spots, often with dark grey centres. Leaves may wither and die.
○ Pick off and burn infected leaves. Improve the feeding and watering regime. It should not be necessary to use a fungicide.

• *Powdery mildew* appears as a white fungal layer, mainly on the upperside of leaves. The foliage may turn purplish red and curl.
○ Remove affected leaves. Fruits may be attacked. Spray with either carbendazim, propiconazole or benomyl.

• *Strawberry beetles* are shiny black beetles that nibble the seeds off the fruits, allowing grey mould to enter and cause rotting.
○ Keep the area free of weeds and sink jam jars as traps.

• *Virus diseases* of several types may attack strawberries, the common symptoms being stunting and distortion, followed by poor cropping and gradual deterioration.
○ No cure is yet available and the viruses are easily spread, so remove and burn affected plants. Plant new strawberries on a fresh site. Control aphids as these spread many viruses.

Vine

• *Magnesium deficiency* appears as yellow and then brown discolouration around the leaf margins and between the veins. The older leaves are affected first. Leaves may die, but generally vigour is not reduced greatly. Excessive use of potash may render magnesium unavailable in the soil.
○ Spray the foliage regularly with a solution of Epsom salts (200 g/10 l water or 8 oz/$2^1/_2$ gal) to which a wetter (e.g. soft soap or a few drops of a liquid detergent) has been added.

• *Powdery mildew* develops as white patches on the foliage and sometimes the young shoots. The berries may remain small and hard, covered in a greyish fungal growth which prevents their normal swelling. They may split or crack, and so be attacked by secondary fungi such as grey mould.
○ Keep plants well watered and ensure good air circulation. Remove affected areas. Spray with sulphur, carbendazim or benomyl.

• *Shanking* causes individual berries to shrivel, starting at the stalk end; they fail to colour normally and have a watery flavour.
○ Improve drainage and feed the vine.

65

·6·
General Troubleshooting

Fruit and vegetables can between them be attacked by a wide range of diseases and pests, and can suffer from a variety of disorders, although many of these attack only one particular plant or group of plants which are closely related. There are other problems which are a more general threat to almost all plants. In addition, there are those problems like the fungal rusts which may appear quite similar and which, to a large extent, can be prevented and controlled by using the same control measures. These are often distinct organisms, each of which attack one particular plant or group of plants.

In this chapter you will find information about some of the problems with very wide host ranges and some of the more common groups of problems. In most cases one particular fungicide can be used against any of the various forms of, say, a powdery mildew; similarly, aphids of all types can be controlled using a product which carries a suitable recommendation. Bearing this in mind, there will be mention of a selection of those chemicals which are readily available to control the problems described. It should always be borne in mind, however, that in one or two instances the chemical may perhaps be unsuitable for use on any one particular type of plant. It is therefore essential to check the label very carefully and to ensure that the product is suitable for the specific control you need to achieve.

Aphids

Without a doubt, these pests are one of the most common and widespread we have to deal with – there are over 550 different species of aphids in the UK alone! Aphids is a general term used to describe the insects we commonly know as greenfly and blackfly: in reality their colours are far more wide ranging and, in my garden at least, there are off-white, through green, pink and yellow, with all shades between and including black!

Aphids are very successful pests and breed at a phenomenal rate: in fact, were a single aphid and her offspring allowed to breed unchecked for just a few weeks in the summer, several thousand individuals could be produced. Luckily for us, aphids are likely to be attacked by their own naturally occurring predators and parasites, and so their full reproductive potential is unlikely to be reached. Even so, in a very short space of time aphids can do a great deal of damage to both fruit and vegetables. Common symptoms are leaf puckering and distortion, often combined with discolouration and stunted growth. They also produce a sticky excreta, honeydew, which may attract black sooty mould fungi.

An added danger is that some transmit viruses as they feed. The importance of controlling aphids is therefore twofold and is perhaps one of the most important pest control tasks in the garden.

Aphids are particularly fond of the soft, succulent parts of a plant, and so are often clustered on the young tender growth. Make regular checks and, although numbers build up very rapidly from late spring onwards, always remember that in greenhouses or protected corners of the garden, they may start to breed much earlier in the year.

Many aphids move on from fruit and vegetables in summer to, say, herbaceous plants and weeds, and so it is important to try to control infestations on all plants. Most fruit trees can be treated with a winter wash, which helps to control overwintering eggs.

❍ There are many different chemicals you can use, including malathion, permethrin/heptenophos and those based on soft soaps. The chemical pirimicarb is, however, preferable in many cases as it only kills aphids, without having any significant effect on the populations of beneficial insects such as ladybirds, hoverflies and lacewings.

Ants

Ants are most commonly red-brown, black or yellowish in colour. They do not attack plants directly but their tunnelling activities may loosen soil around the roots of smaller plants, and occasionally wilting may occur during warmer weather. Ants often appear on plants, and it is easy to presume they may do damage, but they are almost always feeding on honeydew (see under Aphids, Scale insects, Whitefly).

❍ They are virtually impossible to eliminate but they can be watered or dusted with HCH, pirimiphos-methyl or permethrin/heptenophos. Break up the nests before drenching.

Birds

Generally birds do more good than harm in a garden, and to most of us they are to be encouraged as they are not only attractive but also play a role in controlling many pests both on plants and in the soil. A few can, however, cause quite significant damage by consuming buds, leaves, fruits, and young seedlings. Pigeons, for example, rip and eat many vegetables, particularly brassicas, beans and peas and, less frequently, attack bush fruits. Sparrows are attracted to the bright flowers on runner beans and may reduce them to shreds. Bullfinches consume buds on fruit trees, gooseberries and currants. Jays tear open the pods of peas and beans to get at the seeds inside. Starlings sometimes eat a cherry tree almost bare of fruit. Thrushes and blackbirds are also fond of fruit, but generally prefer it when ripe, and can also damage apples, pears, currants and strawberries. In this case they may leave most of the fruit behind, but once pecked it is not only less appetizing, it is

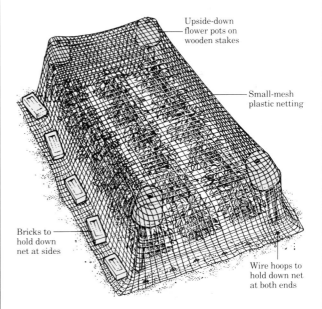

Upside-down flower pots on wooden stakes

Small-mesh plastic netting

Bricks to hold down net at sides

Wire hoops to hold down net at both ends

Fig. 21 A temporary fruit cage can be quickly and simply constructed and, although the netting will need to be removed for spraying or picking, it keeps birds and squirrels at bay.

◄A large walk-in fruit cage can protect all your fruit.

► The bright orange pustules of coral spot appear on dead wood.

also far more prone to attack by fungal infections such as grey mould (especially strawberries – see page 65) or brown rot (top fruit including apples, pears, apricots – see pages 51, 60 and 55). These diseases can very rapidly reduce the crop to a worthless (and often brown, mushy) state!

○ Use barriers to keep birds off vulnerable plants – nets and chicken wire do a good job, provided you keep them taut and make sure there are no gaps. For smaller plants or young crops, drive sticks or canes into the ground and weave cotton between them. Try using a variety of different scarers but remember that, even if you change them and move them around frequently, they soon lose their effectiveness. Erect humming lines. Fruit cages come in a huge range of sizes and shapes – from the larger walk-in types which can contain almost any fruit, to the low cages produced especially for soft fruit growing (Fig. 21), and the wall cage which fits neatly over fan-trained fruits. However you use them, they are a real boon! Their main function is to protect the crop from the ravages of birds, but they also provide some protection against other pest animals, such as squirrels and even rabbits. With a fruit cage the chances of producing a good, undamaged crop are greatly increased.

Bitterness

Fruits may develop a bitterness as a result of unsuitable growing conditions. Poor nutrition, and overwatering are often responsible. Occasionally erratic or insufficient moisture at the roots may also be involved. Excessive use of nitrogen fertilizers, or the planting of crops in ground with a high nitrogen content, is the most common cause.

Cucumbers are particularly prone to bitterness: if they are pollinated they will produce bitter fruits, and those grown outside are also likely to become bitter with age.

Bolting

Lettuces and cabbages are particularly prone to bolting and, before they heart up properly, they go to seed. This premature flowering is usually caused by some check in growth such as drought, or lack of food. Hot, dry summers therefore bring great problems with bolting and a wide range of crops may be affected, including Chinese cabbage, leeks, radish, beetroot and spinach. A sudden change in the temperature can also be responsible, as well as sowing or transplanting either too early or too late.

○ Once the plant has started to flower there is nothing you can do, but in future and with the remainder of the crop, try to avoid or counteract any of the factors which encourage it.

Coral spot

This must be one of the easiest diseases to recognize: it attacks woody plants and also dead woody material such as pea sticks, and produces bright red or coral-coloured raised spots all over the dead area. It once seemed only capable of invading dead wood or, at worst, moving from an area of dead wood into the adjacent living tissue. It would now seem that it has developed more aggressive strains which are quite capable of causing damage in their own right. Currants, figs and gooseberries are

particularly susceptible, but most woody fruit trees or bushes are sometimes attacked. Infection occurs when the spores land on wounds such as those caused by pruning, frost or irregular growth cracks, and the fresher the wound is, the more likely are problems. The pustules themselves only appear once the woody stem has been dead for some time and so they will not be visible initially, which may mean that the disease goes unnoticed and therefore untreated for some time.
❍ Avoid unnecessary injury to plants. Prune out dead or dying stems and remove woody debris in the garden. Infected stems should be pruned out to a point 15 cm (6 in) or more below where it is obviously infected. Use a wound paint on larger pruning wounds (see page 51).

Damping off
Several microscopic soil- or water-borne fungi may be responsible and they attack the roots or stem bases of seedlings shortly after germination has occurred. Affected seedlings wilt and keel over or collapse, and may be covered in fungal growth. To a large extent this problem can be avoided or prevented:
❍ Use only sterilized compost and new or disinfected trays and pots.
❍ Water with mains water, never that collected from a water butt.
❍ Raise seedlings in the conditions stated on the seed packet, taking care not to sow seeds too thickly or keep temperatures too high for too long.
❍ Remove trays from the propagator as soon as germination has occurred and provide plenty of daylight.
❍ Water compost with copper-based fungicide before sowing and then at the stated intervals after germination has occurred.
❍ Prick out carefully, avoiding any injury to the seedling and again ensure strict hygiene.

Regular watering is a must for all fruit and vegetables. If you can't water as frequently as you should, make sure you dig in plenty of bulky material before planting and apply a thick mulch when the soil is really moist.

Foot and root rots
Affected plants show deterioration towards the stem base (foot rot) and/or of the roots (root rots). They soon start to die back and wilt or wither, and then die fairly rapidly, with the lower leaves being the first to show signs of deterioration. Many plants may be affected but tomatoes (page 27), peas (page 41), beans (page 31), aubergines (page 47), peppers (page 47) and cucumbers (page 26) seem particularly susceptible. A similar range of fungi to those causing damping off may be responsible. Plants in containers are often affected, as are those growing in areas previously used for the same or a closely related crop.
❍ Ensure sterilized compost is used, or that crop rotation is practised.
❍ In greenhouse borders, change the soil before replanting.
❍ Use only mains water and avoid overwatering as this too can encourage the disease.
❍ If the disease appears towards the end of the season, it may be worth trying to keep the plants alive and nurtured, just so more of the crop can be produced.
❍ Regularly foliar feed as this will boost vigour and is also believed to encourage root development.
❍ Build up the soil level slightly around the bases of plants like tomatoes, as this may encourage the development of more roots on the stems and so help give protection.

70

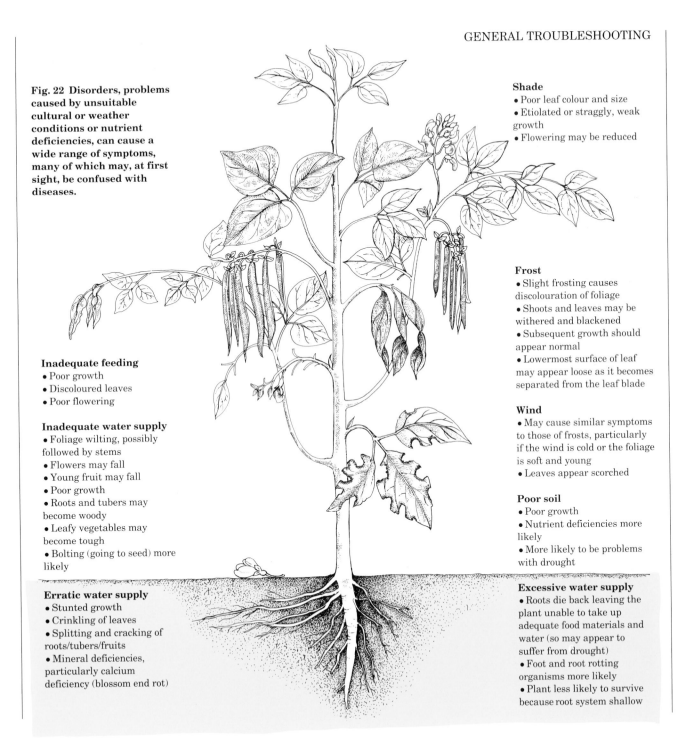

Fig. 22 Disorders, problems caused by unsuitable cultural or weather conditions or nutrient deficiencies, can cause a wide range of symptoms, many of which may, at first sight, be confused with diseases.

Shade
- Poor leaf colour and size
- Etiolated or straggly, weak growth
- Flowering may be reduced

Frost
- Slight frosting causes discolouration of foliage
- Shoots and leaves may be withered and blackened
- Subsequent growth should appear normal
- Lowermost surface of leaf may appear loose as it becomes separated from the leaf blade

Wind
- May cause similar symptoms to those of frosts, particularly if the wind is cold or the foliage is soft and young
- Leaves appear scorched

Poor soil
- Poor growth
- Nutrient deficiencies more likely
- More likely to be problems with drought

Inadequate feeding
- Poor growth
- Discoloured leaves
- Poor flowering

Inadequate water supply
- Foliage wilting, possibly followed by stems
- Flowers may fall
- Young fruit may fall
- Poor growth
- Roots and tubers may become woody
- Leafy vegetables may become tough
- Bolting (going to seed) more likely

Erratic water supply
- Stunted growth
- Crinkling of leaves
- Splitting and cracking of roots/tubers/fruits
- Mineral deficiencies, particularly calcium deficiency (blossom end rot)

Excessive water supply
- Roots die back leaving the plant unable to take up adequate food materials and water (so may appear to suffer from drought)
- Foot and root rotting organisms more likely
- Plant less likely to survive because root system shallow

71

Frost damage

It is always hard to know when frost may strike, even if you listen to the weather forecasts regularly; yet, if insufficient protection is given, frost can cause a lot of damage. Late frost which may occur when there is plenty of new growth around, or when plants are in flower, is generally the most damaging. The crop of a plum tree may be reduced to nothing as a result of frost killing the blossom. Frosts may also cause discolouration of the foliage and cracking of stems – which may in turn allow the entry of other pathogens later on. Leaf distortion is a common symptom too, with the lower-most surface of the leaf sometimes lifting and giving it a strange white or silvery appearance. Soft growth such as new shoots on asparagus (see page 46) may turn black when frosted, but later growth should develop normally.

❍ Site susceptible plants carefully and, of course, avoid frost pockets.
❍ Plant late-flowering fruit as this is more likely to escape damage.
❍ Cut out severely injured areas.
❍ Try overhead watering last thing at night, as this often restricts damage.
❍ Provide protection where possible: dry straw, sacking or spun polypropylene fleece can be laid over crops or wound around soft stems.

Grey mould

Grey mould can be found on almost all plants and on plant debris left around the garden or greenhouse. Infected areas often turn brown and soft and are covered in a dense fuzzy grey fungal growth which bears hundreds of spores. These are easily spread on air currents, by contact, and by water or rain splash. Fruits such as raspberries (see

◄ **Distorted and blackened stems and leaves are a common symptom of frost.**

Mice can easily climb up and eat the cobs of sweet corn.

page 63) and frequently strawberries (see page 65) are rapidly reduced to a brown pulpy (and totally inedible) mass. Lettuces (see page 26) are often attacked, and the butt or head turns brown and soft. Even woody stems can be attacked and in some cases extensive deterioration may occur (e.g. 'gooseberry dieback'). If spores land on unripe tomatoes they may produce 'ghost spotting' where white or yellow circles appear on the fruit which remains otherwise unaffected.

❍ Always ensure good hygiene and clear up any deteriorating plant material immediately.
❍ Improve air circulation and avoid stagnant conditions at all costs.
❍ Remove infected areas promptly, where appropriate, pruning back into completely sound growth.
❍ Avoid overhead watering as this may spread many spores rapidly.
❍ Avoid unnecessary injury as infection often occurs via injured areas – remember to keep slugs and birds away from crops.

○ Spray with carbendazim, benomyl or thiophanate-methyl. Check label particularly carefully as in some cases (e.g. for strawberries) spraying may be advisable well before infection is actually seen.

Honey fungus (Fig. 23)

Without doubt, this is the gardener's nightmare! Honey fungus can, potentially, attack most woody plants and usually causes obvious deterioration followed by death within a year or two. Occasionally decline may be more rapid than this. In the autumn clusters of honey-coloured toadstools may appear around the base of infected plants. The infection itself, however, occurs under ground – specially toughened black fungal strands (rhizomorphs or bootlaces) grow from a source of infection and penetrate the bark at the trunk/stem base or on the larger roots. Sometimes healthy roots come into

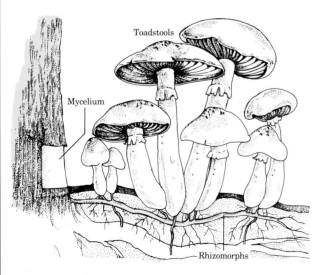

Fig. 23 Honey fungus rhizomorphs travel through the soil, penetrate the bark and form a compact, creamy-white fungal sheet (mycelium) under the bark. Toadstools may be formed in the autumn.

> ## · COMMON VICTIMS OF HONEY FUNGUS ·
>
> ● *Edible and ornamental: Malus* (flowering crabs and apples), *Prunus* (ornamental and edible, including plum, cherry, damson, peach, apricot, almond), *Pyrus* (pears and ornamental species), *Ribes* (edible currants and flowering currants, gooseberries), *Rubus* (raspberries, blackberries, loganberries), *Vitis* (grapes and ornamental species)
>
> ● *Other ornamentals* which are often attacked include: Araucaria, birch, cedar, cotoneaster, cypress, forsythia, hydrangea, laburnum, lilac, maple, paeony, pine, privet, rhododendron, rose, spruce, viburnum, willow, wisteria

contact with buried sources of infection such as infected roots, old stumps and so on, and this too can cause them to become infected.

To check for honey fungus carefully expose a few larger roots or lift small areas of bark: if infection has occurred a white fungal sheet (mycelium) will be found sandwiched between the bark and the wood of the root. Adjacent tissue may be rotted, often with a wet, spongy texture. Occasionally rhizomorphs may be found under the bark too. A similar inspection could also be carried out at the base of the stem/trunk.

○ Remove infected plants, together with their stumps and as much root as possible – leave this in and you leave behind a dangerous source of infection!

○ Vigorous, well-maintained plants seem less prone to infection and so ensure everything is kept in prime condition!

Old age

There comes a time when everything starts to show signs of age. The symptoms vary from plant to plant but expect to see poor growth, often with small or slightly discoloured leaves and poor fruiting. There are many possible reasons for the appearance of any of these problems but generally, if you know the age of the plant and feel it may be nearing its end, and find that it seems free from diseases and pests and that feeding and nurturing have little effect, then old age is probably responsible. It can be very difficult removing an 'old friend' which has cropped well for many years but, if you can, do try to be hard-hearted and take it out. There are always new varieties as well as the old favourites to choose from for a replacement.

One important thing to remember is that you must never try to grow the same or a closely related plant in the old site as this may cause 'replant' problems – your new fruit will never really thrive and indeed may gradually decline for no apparent reason. If a completely new site is not available, then you may succeed if you change the soil in the area to the depth and spread of the old root systems and a little bit further.

Red spider mite

In hot, dry summers red spider mite (now more correctly known as the two-spotted mite) will damage plants growing outside but it is best known for the devastation it can cause to plants growing in greenhouses. The tiny mites (visible with the aid of a hand lens) are a pale brownish green with black markings and feed by sucking plant sap. Their numbers build up rapidly and clear signs of damage soon appear as the foliage is covered with fine, dense yellowish white flecking. This is soon followed by drying and browning of the leaves. When their population levels are high, fine silken webbing may be seen draped over the infested plant. If left unchecked the plant may be killed. Cucumbers, melons, aubergines and peaches are most frequently attacked.

○ If you are to achieve any measure of success when controlling these pests, you must start early! Try to keep temperatures relatively low and keep air humid by regularly drenching the floor of the greenhouse and misting the foliage – the mites hate getting wet!
○ Several proprietary sprays are available but check the labels carefully as they are not all suitable for use on every type of plant: malathion, pyrethrum, pirimiphos-methyl, derris and fatty acids.
○ Consider biological control using the predatory mite *Phytoseiulus persimilis*.

Rodents

Mice and squirrels may cause different types of damage to a wide range of fruit and vegetables. The plants most commonly attacked are peas, beans (the seeds are dug up and removed, or eaten shortly after sowing), fruit and nut trees and bushes (fruits, berries and nuts are eaten or nibbled, and bark may occasionally be chewed off stems and trunks), and fruits and vegetables in store (nibbled or eaten).
○ Mice may be caught in traps or killed using poisons and baits.
○ Squirrels and mice may be kept off the susceptible plants to a certain extent by the use of barriers such as fine-mesh galvanized wire netting.
○ Invest in a fruit cage (see page 68) as this will not only keep the squirrels out but also the birds.

Rusts

The leaves of some fruit and vegetables may be attacked by rust fungi, each rust usually only attacking one particular crop or group of closely related plants. Those commonly affected include beetroot, beans, leeks, chives, mint, plums, raspberries and blackberries. The upper surface of the leaves show yellow spots or blotches, and if you turn the leaves over you find patches or pustules of

◄ Honey fungus toadstools only appear in autumn and usually grow in groups. They have honey-coloured caps often with dark brown flecking and their stems bear a tiny 'collar'. They produce white spores.

orange or blackish-brown spores. Affected leaves discolour and may wither and die back. With mint the stems are severely contorted as a result of the infection which occurs along their length. Occasionally cane infections may be seen on raspberries and blackberries too. Rust fungi thrive in moist conditions so they are likely to be more of a problem in wet summers, or towards the end of the summer when there is usually more rain. In some cases, for instance with plums, infection is therefore of no great significance as the leaves only fall slightly earlier than normal and the tree is not severely weakened.

○ Infected areas should always be removed as soon as possible or, in the case of large plants, infected leaves should be raked up as soon as they fall.

○ Try to improve air circulation around the plants by good spacing, pruning (where appropriate), and the removal of weeds.

○ Avoid excessive use of high-nitrogen fertilizers and dress the soil with sulphate of potash before sowing/planting out.

○ Remove all debris at the end of the season and, where appropriate, rotate crops.

Scale insects
Strange, waxy yellowish, grey or dark brown, elliptical or rounded insects, with no visible legs, antennae or eyes, attack the stems or leaves of some fruits. They are usually found in groups, often clustered on the stems or on the underside of the leaves, close to the veins. They suck the plant sap

▲ Scale insects may blend in quite well with the stems or foliage on which they feed.

◄ A heavy infestation of red spider mite causes the foliage to discolour and the plants become draped in silken webbing.

77

and may excrete large quantities of sticky, sugary honeydew, causing sticky patches to develop. This honeydew may later be colonized by black sooty mould fungi which are harmless to the plant but which cause an unsightly black deposit to develop.

○ Dormant fruit trees and bushes can be sprayed with a winter wash. Spray infested plants with malathion, pyrethrum, pirimiphos-methyl or fatty acid spray. Clean infested bark with a scrubbing brush and water.

Slugs and snails

It seems that whatever you do, slugs and snails still cause problems, eating ragged holes in the foliage of plants, causing most damage close to ground level but also sometimes attacking stems and fruits (particularly on strawberries). Most feeding is done after dusk, and during damper weather it may be

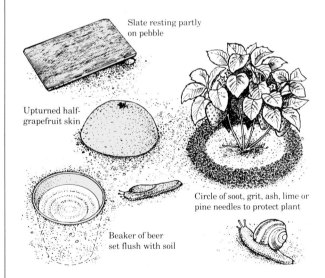

Slate resting partly on pebble

Upturned half-grapefruit skin

Circle of soot, grit, ash, lime or pine needles to protect plant

Beaker of beer set flush with soil

Fig. 24 Home-made slug traps can be very effective – try upturned half-grapefruit skins, slates or beakers of beer. Circles of ash, soot, grit, lime or pine needles around plants may prevent slugs from reaching them.

possible to see large numbers of these pests. Look for the characteristic silvery slime trail which will remain long after the pest itself has gone. Smaller keeled slugs feed on underground plant parts and can ruin a crop of potatoes very rapidly. Try to minimize their potential hiding places such as heaps of organic matter, rubble, stones,etc. Check any such places regularly and collect any hiding slugs and snails.

○ Over the years numerous ideas have been developed which help to keep slug numbers down. The effectiveness of these cannot always be guaranteed, but they can frequently greatly decrease the number of slugs attacking your plants. You could try traps – upturned grapefruit skins, large brassica leaves, or even pieces of slate, all of which will lure the slugs for you then to collect up and destroy; underground traps made from plastic beakers full of beer, which draw the slugs into the beaker where they then drown; physical barriers to protect the plants, such as sections of clear plastic drinks bottles, circles of soot, lime, pine needles around the base of the plant (Fig. 24).

○ As a final resort, try a proprietary slug killer, such as slug pellets based on metaldehyde or methiocarb, or products based on aluminium sulphate. Use more than once, as recommended by the manufacturer.

Suckers (apple and pear)

Leaf and blossom buds, and later the older foliage, may be attacked by these pests, causing it to become discoloured and distorted. Blossom may fail to develop normally and so the crop may be affected.

○ Spray with dimethoate.

Wind damage/spray damage

Leaves can be scorched by strong winds, especially if the foliage is still fairly tender, or if the plant is in rather an exposed position. In extreme cases smaller

· HANDY TIP ·

Rubbish or debris left lying around in the garden or greenhouse not only looks unsightly but may also act as a superb hiding, breeding or over-wintering place for pests. Have good, regular spring cleaning sessions, in spring, summer, autumn and winter.

shoots or stems may even die back. Fruiting may be reduced not only by damage to the flowers but also because the numbers of pollinating insects is affected by very strong winds. In extreme cases a tree may actually develop a lopsided appearance, but if this happens it really is a case of bad positioning!

❍ Plant in less exposed sites and create barriers such as hedges to decrease wind damage.

Chemical sprays, particularly weedkillers can contaminate fruit and vegetables. The exact symptoms seen are determined by both the spray used and the plant damaged. Common symptoms include distortion of the foliage and new growth, and the production of thickened, almost strap-like leaves, outgrowths on stems (especially on brassicas) and the production of hollow, elongated fruits (tomatoes). In general, affected plants will recover and growth produced later in the season should be perfectly normal. However, the appearance of the plants and the cropping may be severely affected.

❍ Take extreme care when using weedkillers and always follow closely the instructions with regards to safety, suitable times and weather conditions. Never spray on hot or windy days and always keep one applicator for using solely with weedkillers. Use a watering-can with dribble bar attachment in preference to a sprayer as this is less likely to allow drift. Do not use fresh lawn clippings from a lawn treated with weedkiller.

Whitefly

Another unmistakable pest – disturb infested plants in a greenhouse and the whitefly fly up in clouds. These tiny white creatures look rather like miniature moths and feed by sucking plant sap. They are especially troublesome in greenhouses and the plants get covered in large quantities of sticky honeydew which later becomes colonized by the harmless but unsightly black sooty mould fungi. The pests are most prevalent on the undersides of infested leaves and will be found clustered together. Pale yellow, flattened, elliptical nymphs or scales (less than 1 mm in length) are also located on the undersurface of the leaves; these develop into pupae from which the adult whitefly emerge. Whitefly breed rapidly and in warm conditions their life cycle is completed in only three weeks. Tomatoes and cucumbers are particularly prone to attack. If allowed to feed and breed unchecked, the foliage of infested plants will yellow and wither.

❍ Try spraying with permethrin, pirimiphos-methyl, pyrethrum or fatty acid spray. Alternatively, you could consider using biological control by introducing the parasitic wasp *Encarsia formosa*.

Woodlice

These creatures feed mainly on rotting vegetation but may attack seedlings and young shoot tips, and foliage. They are very partial to strawberries. They nibble irregular holes in the leaves and with seedlings, may attack them at soil level, so causing them to keel over. They are a greyish colour, and have segmented bodies; they may be up to 2 cm ($^3/_4$ in) in length and have up to seven pairs of legs. They feed mainly at night and during the day they seek cover under pots, stones and in similarly protected places.

❍ Dust with gamma-BHC (HCH). Remove hiding places.

· 7 ·
Chemical v. Organic

Among all gardeners there are those who refuse to use any sort of chemical fertilizer or pesticide, while at the other extreme there are those who perhaps rely rather too heavily on garden chemicals and expect them to do all the hard work for them! Between these two groups lie the majority of us who are aware of what good gardening means (even if they are sometimes a bit reluctant to practise it!), who try to keep pest and disease problems at bay by growing crops under good conditions and maintaining them in the right way, but who will also resort to using chemicals when necessary.

Whichever group you feel you fall into, the chances are that you will have thought, albeit briefly, about the 'chemical versus organic' argument. On the organic side is the worry that use of chemicals is dangerous because they could produce nasty side effects either now or in the future; also that they leave harmful residues on fruit and vegetables; and that they are not sufficiently selective to leave all the harmless or even beneficial creatures un-harmed. Admittedly there have been occasions where chemicals have been withdrawn after being used for many years, or when there have been reports of a particular chemical having been found to possess carcinogenic properties. However, it is worth remembering that the testing and legislation surrounding chemical production and sales is now very extensive and takes into account not only the chemical's ability to do the job but also its safety to both the user, wildlife and the environment in general. With regard to residues, on every chemical product you should find a clearly stated time period which you must wait between spraying and eating the produce. Once this 'harvest period' has elapsed, the crop is said to be perfectly safe to eat and any residues left should cause no harm.

I feel sure that most of the worries concerning chemical products stem from scare stories and cases where they have been misused – in other words, not used according to the instructions. It is abuse rather than sensible, reasoned use of chemicals which has, in my opinion, given them a bad name. Admittedly there have been occasional problems, but then there is some danger in everything – from using garden tools, handling certain plants, or even using some of the 'organic' products.

For myself, I choose to concentrate mainly on preventing problems, combined with good garden hygiene and a frame of mind which does not expect or seek perfection, so puts up with the odd small blemish on my fruit and vegetables. But there are certainly times when I find chemicals are a great help and the only answer to keeping the crop in reasonable condition. It is this balance, including sensible and careful use of chemicals, which I find provides me with what I want.

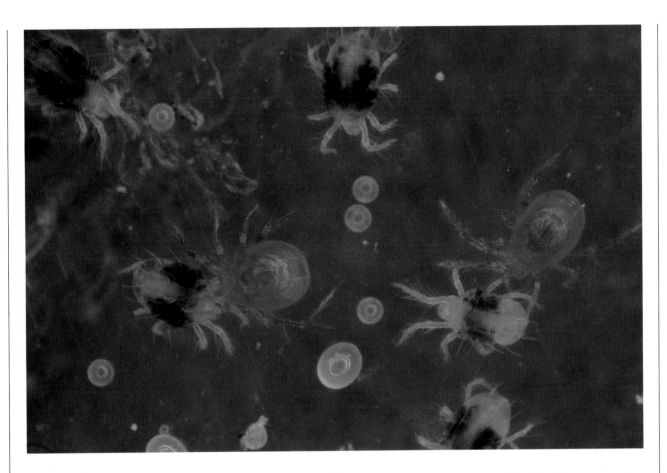

Chemical formulations

As it is all too easy to see in a garden centre, most garden chemicals can be purchased in a range of different packaging, and often in one or more different formulations. It is the chemical constituents of the pesticide which determines how it works, which problems it should be used against, the timing and frequency of applications needed for success and, of course, whether it is suitable for use on the plant you have in mind. However, the way in which it has been formulated may have influence too and affects how easy it is to use and how effective it is likely to be.

The types of formulation most frequently seen on sale are liquids, wettable powders, dusts, smokes

Despite their common name, red spider mites are usually yellowish green. The predatory mite *Phytoseiulus* is reddish orange.

and baits, as well as ready-to-use liquids which do not even need to be diluted before use. The type you choose may be determined by strong personal preference, but always consider factors such as price and convenience, range of other purposes it could serve, and of course suitability.

Safe use of chemicals

Whatever you buy and wherever you use it, you must only use a chemical for the purposes and in the way described by the manufacturer. Information

81

like this is given clearly on the pack of all products and is occasionally supplemented by further facts on a printed sheet found within the box. You'll find that by sticking to this rule you will not only be keeping within the law, but also making the product more effective and avoiding any unnecessary complications or trouble.

● *The basic rules* for safe use of chemicals are:

1. Choose the right chemical for the purpose you have in mind.

2. Think before applying it – is it really necessary?

3. Spray on a suitable day, that is avoid windy or very hot weather – both allow spray drift.

4. Spray in the early morning or evening (this reduces the risk of damage to the plants themselves and to pollinating insects).

5. Use it at precisely the rate, time and frequency stated on the label (never feel inclined to add that little bit extra, or to cut corners!).

6. Only mix chemicals if the manufacturer advises this, and then only with the products stated on the pack.

7. Apply the product very carefully, avoiding inhaling dusts or smokes, and avoiding contact with the skin or eyes.

8. Keep children and pets out of the newly treated area (see pack for details).

9. Never drink, eat or smoke while applying any pesticide, and always wash your hands well afterwards.

10. Keep chemicals out of reach of small children, preferably in a locked cupboard in their original packaging, together with any additional information about the product.

Disposal of chemicals
Always try to make up the correct amount of spray so that you are not left with large quantities of unwanted chemical for which you have no use – this is both wasteful and leaves you with the problem of how and where to get rid of it. If you do find you have left-over chemical at any time, you should spray it onto bare ground or onto other plants on which it could have safely been used. Do not feel tempted to tip it down the drain or the lavatory.

If you discover a collection of old or leaking packs of garden chemicals in the back of your shed, your local council should be able to advise you on the facilities they can offer for their safe disposal.

USING BIOLOGICAL CONTROLS

Apart from that which occurs naturally in the garden, biological control is really most suitable on fruit or vegetables growing in greenhouses. If you grow ornamentals in your greenhouse you will also find it can be used to control pest problems on these just as effectively too.

If you want to try biological control it is always advisable to introduce the predators or parasites when the pests have arrived (so that there is something for the biological control agents to feed on) but before the pest population is too high (so that the beneficial creatures don't have too much of an uphill struggle and can increase rapidly enough to keep the pests at bay). In addition there are minimum temperature requirements needed for good activity and breeding of the biological control agents. Full details of these conditions are given when they are obtained, usually by mail order.

Aphids
There are two possible solutions to aphids: a predatory midge called *Aphidoletes* and a parasitic wasp called *Aphidius*. The midges lay their red eggs

on the foliage of the greenhouse plants after dark. After three or four days these hatch and produce a pale orange larva which may be up to 3 mm in length. Each larva attacks aphids by gripping onto a leg joint and then sucking out all its body contents. Each larva is believed to feed on in excess of 60 aphids. The parasitic wasp's larva develops within a living aphid, kills it and mummifies the body, producing a rigid buff-coloured shell, out of which it emerges when its development is complete.
❍ Chemical alternatives are pirimicarb, heptenophos with permethrin, pyrethrum, insecticidal soaps.

Caterpillars

These pests can be controlled using biological control either outside or in the greenhouse. A biological insecticide containing bacteria called *Bacillus thuringiensis* can be sprayed onto plants which are under attack from caterpillars, and when the caterpillar eats foliage it dies because it succumbs to the bacterial infection. The bacteria are only damaging to caterpillars so pose no threat to other living organisms.
❍ Chemical alternatives are permethrin, derris, fenitrothion, pirimiphos-methyl.

Glasshouse whitefly

These can be kept at an extremely low level using a minute parasitic wasp called *Encarsia formosa*. This tiny creature is about 0.6 mm long, so only just visible to the naked eye. Each lays up to 100 eggs, placing one in each of the nymphal stage (scale) of the whitefly, on which it feeds. The egg hatches to produce a grub which feeds on the developing whitefly, kills it, and causes the scale to turn black. The adult wasp then cuts a circular exit hole in the blackened scale and emerges to start the process off all over again.

An added benefit is that the adult wasps eat the sticky honeydew excreted by the whitefly and so help cut down the development of black sooty mould which grows on the honeydew.
❍ Chemical alternatives are permethrin, pyrethrum, pirimiphos-methyl, insecticidal soaps.

Mealy bugs

These can be controlled using a relative of the ladybird, called *Cryptolaemus*. The adult beetles are about 3.5 mm long and have a blackish body with a dark red head and thorax. They readily fly off, so after introducing them into the greenhouse, keep the vents, windows and doors shut for several hours until they get used to their surroundings. Their larvae look rather like out-size mealy bugs. Both the adults and the larvae are voracious feeders and soon devour the clumps of mealy bugs.
❍ Chemical alternatives are malathion, dimethoate, pirimiphos-methyl.

Two-spotted mite (red spider mite)

This pest and its eggs can be controlled by a predatory mite called *Phytoseiulus persimilis*. The predator is similar in size to the pest but has a much more rounded body and is a reddish-orange colour (despite its name, red spider mite is actually a browny-yellow colour!) Again they can just be seen with the naked eye, but a hand lens makes for much easier viewing. The predators run extremely fast and feed on all stages of the red spider mite, including its eggs.
❍ Chemical alternatives are malathion, derris, dimethoate, pirimiphos-methyl, insecticidal soaps.

·8·

Storage

Even the most carefully planned kitchen garden will sometimes produce a glut of one or more crops, and rather than eating far too much or wasting the produce it seems only sensible to store as much as possible. Some vegetables, like lettuces, are really only suitable for short-term storage in a refrigerator, but almost everything else can have its useful life prolonged tremendously if stored, by either clamping, boxing, bagging or freezing (Fig. 25). Each method has crops best suited to it and, although they may sound complicated at first, it is easy to get into the swing of things and soon find that your home-grown fruit and vegetables can last much longer.

Clamping

This is particularly suitable for root crops, (especially potatoes, but occasionally carrots and turnips too) and ensures that they are protected from frost and excessively wet soil conditions. The clamp is constructed on freely draining soil. The crop is arranged in a steeply sloping conical heap and surrounded on all sides and the base by a 30 cm (12 in) layer of straw. This insulating layer is then surrounded by a 23 cm (9 in) deep layer of fine soil which is tamped well down. Generally clamps are built to a height of about 1 m ($3^{1}/_{4}$ ft). To provide some ventilation, carefully pull a handful of straw out from the ridge of the cone so that it protrudes in a tuft. This moist air escapes and so decreases the chances of the crops deteriorating.

Boxes

This is one of the simplest methods of storage. The crops are lifted and placed in wooden boxes full of dry sand or light, dry soil. They can then be placed in a frost-free shed or even a garage. This method is most often used for Jerusalem artichokes, beetroot, carrots, celeriac, parsnips, radishes, salsify, scorzonera, swedes and turnips. Any foliage should be carefully trimmed back before storage, as it may otherwise start to rot and could subsequently damage the stored crops.

Bagging

This method is often used for storing marrows. Young marrows are less likely to keep well, so choose fully mature ones which have ripened completely. All that you need do is put each one in an individual net or string bag and then hang it in a frost-free shed or garage. If you do not already have nets, a very cheap substitute can be made from sections of nylon stockings or tights.

Ropes

Onions and garlic are not only suited to being roped, but once you have managed to construct each rope

▶ One of the easiest ways to store carrots is to build a clamp and, if you have no shed, cool greenhouse or garage, it is a method you will need to rely on.

84

1. The base of the carrot clamp is formed by laying a circle of carrots on the soil.

2. Carrots are added layer by layer, the largest at the base the smallest at the top to form a pyramid.

3. A layer of dry straw is laid over the entire surface of the pyramid.

4. Finally a layer of garden soil is firmed down over the straw, completing the clamp.

Fig. 25 Clamping, drying, netting and boxing are useful methods of storage when you have a glut of fruit or vegetables.

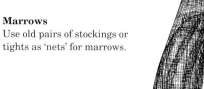

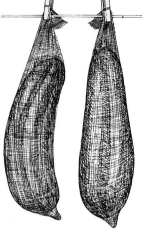

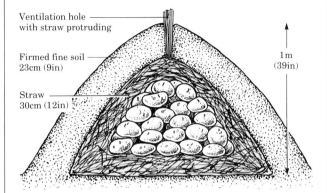

Ventilation hole
with straw protruding

Firmed fine soil
23cm (9in)

Straw
30cm (12in)

1m
(39in)

Potatoes, carrots and turnips

Use clamps and always ensure that only completely healthy and unmarked tubers are stored. Inspect each one carefully and do not use any which have been damaged on lifting.

Onions and garlic

With a bit of patience, practice and a length of raffia, you can plait your onions and garlic into traditional 'strings'.

Marrows

Use old pairs of stockings or tights as 'nets' for marrows.

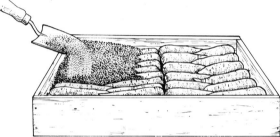

Root vegetables

Wooden boxes from the greengrocer can be used as mini-crates for storage. Loosely pack the trimmed root vegetables between layers of dry sand or light dry soil and store in a cool but frost-free shed.

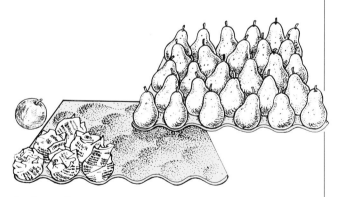

Apples and pears

Papier-mâché or polystyrene trays from the greengrocers are excellent storage trays for apples and pears. Wrap each apple in a piece of newspaper, but do not wrap pears.

you will find that it also has great potential as a gift, and of course looks rather attractive hanging in a cool spot in your own kitchen!

Once the onions are dried off (usually about 2 weeks after lifting), all you need do is carefully plait them into a sturdy string, using raffia plaited in too, to ensure it is strong enough to carry the weight.

Freezing

If freezing is done well and the produce is really freshly picked, the lovely taste and texture of your favourite fruit and vegetables need hardly suffer at all. Always try to freeze the crops as soon as possible and always choose the very best as better quality produce will freeze the best. Many vegetables can be blanched, but this practice is now often considered unnecessary for really fresh crops.

If you decide to try blanching, use a large saucepan (at least 3 litres/5 pints capacity), and either a special blanching basket or a metal sieve. With about 0.5 kg (1 lb) of vegetables in the basket, plunge it into the boiling water, keep the heat up high and bring the water to the boil again. Most vegetables need to be blanched for between one-and-a-half and three minutes, so for specific details

always check in a specialist freezer book. After blanching, run the vegetables under cold water to stop any further blanching.

Most vegetables are best frozen singly, so spread them out on a tray then, once frozen, they can be put together into tightly sealed plastic bags or freezer boxes. Always try to keep the air in the bag or box to a minimum.

Fruit is easier to freeze as it never needs blanching. Almost all the fruit you could think of growing in your garden can be frozen successfully, with two well-known exceptions being pears and strawberries. Fruit can be frozen fresh as soon as it is picked, or sliced and layered with sugar or stewed.

Trays

Mid- or late-season apples can be stored on trays for anything from a few weeks to several months, depending on the cultivar. The store must be frost-free, rodent-proof, dark, cool and with both reasonable levels of humidity and adequate air circulation; a shed, cellar or even a garage is usually suitable. Pears may be stored in similar conditions but rarely last very long. If kept in the vegetable compartment of a fridge they may, however, keep very well.

Store medium-sized, healthy looking fruits in wooden fruit trays (often available from your local greengrocer or market), or in the moulded papier-mache or polystyrene trays which are placed on

Crop	Length of time (in minutes)	Crop	Length of time (in minutes)
Asparagus	2–3	Courgette	2
Bean		Leek	1–$\frac{1}{2}$
● broad	1–1$\frac{1}{2}$	Parsnip	2
● French	2 (sliced)	Pea	1
	or 3 (whole)	Potato, new	3
● runner	2	Salsify	2
Broccoli	3	Scorzonera	2
Brussels sprout	2$\frac{1}{2}$–3	Spinach	2
Carrot	2 (young)	Sweet corn	3 (small)
	or 3 (old)	(whole cob)	6 (large)

· BLANCHING TIMES ·

slatted shelves within the store (to allow good air circulation and to keep each fruit separate from its neighbours). Apples tend to keep slightly longer and are less prone to becoming wrinkled due to moisture loss if each one is wrapped in its own piece of newspaper. Pears should not be wrapped.

Polythene bags

If you have no room for a special store, or have only a few apples which need to be stored, try the extremely simple method using polythene bags. Put about 2 kg (4½ lb) of apples in each clear polythene bag and fold the top over (do not seal it tightly). Then, to ensure that there is adequate air circulation, use a pencil to make four or five well-spaced holes in the polythene. Although this method does work exceptionally well, there is a greater chance of storage rots developing, so examine each bag frequently.

Apples can be stored in a polythene bag, but first make several holes in the bag with a pencil.

·9·
Calendar

The very concept of spraying to prevent any disease or pest attacking your fruit, or at least to minimize any possible damage, is not something that will appeal to everyone. Nowadays many gardeners – both those who have many years' experience behind them, and many first timers – have started to think a lot harder before reaching for the sprayer at all.

Preventative spraying of this type means you spray against a range of problems which could *possibly* affect the plant, regardless of whether or not you see the disease or pest, and often regardless of whether or not it has been a problem in previous years. However, the knowledge that there has been extensive pest and/or disease damage in the past often makes the idea of preventative spraying more acceptable to gardeners.

Objections to a fruit-spraying programme

The main objections to a fruit-spraying programme, as far as many gardeners are concerned are as follows:

● *It appears wasteful* as large quantities of chemical may be used, usually several times each season. In order to achieve successful control or prevention of the wide range of pests and diseases which could attack your tree or bush fruit, there will be several different chemicals involved.

● *It can be expensive* – it really is amazing how the cost of several different chemicals will start to add up! If you have only a couple of trees then the cost per tree will, of course, seem even higher. You may find that if you make up the smallest volume of spray you are able to calculate accurately, there is still some left unused after each application – and the problem of disposing any left-over chemical may also concern you.

● *It can be time-consuming*, because of the regular intervals at which each spray needs to be applied throughout the season. Even though it may sometimes prove possible to apply two chemicals together, this is not always so. Always check the label carefully to see whether the chemical you have chosen can be mixed with any other one. If the combination you have in mind is not specified by the manufacturers then do not be tempted to try it.

● *It can be harmful to the environment*, as many sprays are known to have a potentially damaging effect on organisms other than those you are trying to control. Many insecticides, for example, will not only kill a good range of pests, but may also have a damaging effect on local populations of some harmless or even beneficial insects.

Benefits of a fruit-spraying programme

There is no doubt that the benefits of a spraying programme on your fruit are considerable: it really is the most reliable, or perhaps even the only feasible way of producing fruit with the minimum possible number of diseases or pests.

In conclusion, gardeners wishing to produce show-case fruit, or for those who are serious exhibitors at local or even regional shows, then following a spray programme is, perhaps, advisable. On the other hand, for most of us it seems better to use preventative sprays against only those problems which have been repeatedly troublesome and which cannot be adequately controlled on a 'spray as soon as seen' basis.

Flowering stages (Fig. 26)

The stage of development of the buds, flowers and fruitlets is often used as a means by which the timing of applications of sprays can be gauged. The precise appearance of each stage will, of course, be determined largely by the cultivar and the prevailing weather conditions but the following is a general guide.

- *For apples*, the main flowering stages are:
  Dormant – Early to late winter
  Bud burst – Early to mid-spring
  Green cluster – Mid-spring
  Pink bud – Towards late spring
  80% petal fall – Late spring/early summer
  Fruitlet – Early summer

- *For pears*, the main flowering stages are:
  Dormant – Early to mid-winter
  Bud burst – Early spring
  Green cluster – Mid-spring
  White bud – Mid-spring
  80% petal fall – Late spring
  Fruitlet stage – Late spring

- *For plums*, the main flowering stages are:
  Dormant – Early to mid-winter
  White bud – Mid-spring
  Cot split – Late spring

Fig. 26 Flowering stages.

Dormant
Trees can be sprayed with a tar oil winter wash, preferably during early to mid-winter.

Bud burst
As the buds burst (early to mid-spring) the tree can be sprayed to prevent powdery mildew and scab.

Green cluster
When at the green cluster stage, the buds are quite green and the tree can be sprayed with insecticides to control winter moth caterpillars, aphids and apple sucker, and with a fungicide to continue scab and powdery mildew control.

Pink bud
At the pink bud stage, when the buds are nearly ready to open and faintly tinged pink, the fungicide spraying could be continued.

When to spray

Those problems which result in fruit which is spoiled or rendered inedible by severe infestations of pests or attacks of diseases may need more regular spraying. In addition, a pest or disease which greatly reduces the useful or acceptable crop at the end of the season may be something you feel you wish to spray preventatively against. Perhaps there is a local problem with pear midge – with this pest, if you were to wait until you saw signs of the damage then, as far as spraying is concerned, it really is too late anyway.

One of the diseases which most easily wrecks a potentially heavy and mouthwateringly tasty crop of strawberries is grey mould or botrytis. Although the spores readily spread from one infected fruit to another healthy one, the initial outbreaks usually result from infection which took place at flowering time. The grey mould spores arrive when the strawberry is in flower but do not develop on the hard, yellow tiny fruitlets. Instead they remain almost dormant until the fruit starts to ripen. Then, as it begins to turn reddish in colour and its sugar content rises as it starts to ripen, suddenly the spores of the grey mould multiply and burst out from within the fruit, turning it into a soft, pulpy brown mass in no time at all. To avoid this, the only real answer is to spray around flowering time.

Severe attacks of codling moth can also be disastrous as far as the quality of the crop is concerned. Again preventative spraying – combined, of course, with cultural methods – really is the best answer. If the timing of the spraying is calculated with the aid of a pheremone trap, then spraying can be extremely effective.

It is always worth bearing in mind that most problems are strongly influenced by weather conditions and so will not necessarily appear each year. This in itself may mean that there really is no need to spray routinely.

· FRUIT-SPRAYING PROGRAMME ·

Flowering stage	Spraying programme
● APPLE	
Dormant	Spray with winter wash to control scale, suckers, aphids and winter moth eggs
Bud burst	Spray carbendazim, bupirimate with triforine or benomyl to control powdery mildew and scab
Green cluster	Spray with heptenophos and permethrin to control sucker and aphids and caterpillars; repeat fungicide spray
80% petal fall	Repeat fungicide spray; repeat insecticide spray
Pink bud	Repeat fungicide spray; repeat insecticide spray
Fruitlet	Repeat insecticide spray or spray with fenitrothion against codling moth; spray with calcium nitrate to prevent bitter pit
● PEAR	
Dormant	Spray with winter wash against winter moth eggs and aphids
Bud burst	Spray with carbendazim, benomyl, bupirimate with triforine against scab
Green cluster	Repeat fungicide spray
White bud	Repeat fungicide spray; spray with heptenophos and pemethrin to control pear sucker and aphids; spray with fenitrothion or gamma HCH against pear midge
80% petal fall	Repeat fungicide spray
Fruitlet	Repeat fungicide spray
● PLUM	
Dormant	Spray with winter wash against aphids and winter moth eggs
White bud	Spray with heptenophos and permethrin against aphids and caterpillars
Cot split	Spray with heptenophos and permethrin to control aphids and plum sawfly
Late summer, early and mid-autumn	Spray with a copper fungicide against bacterial canker

Ideally each of these programmes should be altered to account for the fact that certain diseases or pests may never or only very rarely appear on your trees. In addition, where the only pests which you wish to spray against are aphids, a spray containing pirimicarb should be used as, unlike other aphicides this does not kill beneficial insects.

Special spray programmes are usually only used against tree fruit, in particular apples, sometimes pears and occasionally plums. Their use on soft fruit is rare but, as mentioned above, there are cases where preventative spraying may indeed prove worthwhile.

▲ Always take great care when mixing and using chemicals and follow the instructions to the letter.

► Tar oil winter wash can be used when the tree is fully dormant. Always protect adjacent grass and other plants.

· ACTIVE INGREDIENTS IN PROPRIETARY PRODUCTS ·

Active ingredient	Proprietary product
● FUNGICIDES	
Benomyl	Benlate (ICI)
Bupirimate with trifoine	Nimrod T (ICI)
Carbendazim	Systemic Action Fungicide (Murphy) Bio Supercarb (pbi)
Copper	Traditional Copper Fungicide (Murphy) Bordeaux Mixture (Vitax)
Copper (suitable only for damping off disease)	Bio Cheshunt Compound (pbi)
Mancozeb	Bio Dithane 945 (pbi)
Propiconazole	Tumbleblite (Murphy)
Sulphur	Green Sulphur (Vitax) Safer's Garden Fungicide (Phostrogen) Bio Friendly Pest and Disease Duster (pbi)
Thiram	Bio Hexyl (pbi)
● INSECTICIDES	
Bacillus thuringiensis	Dipel
Derris	Derris Dust (Murphy, Vitax, Doff, ICI Liquid Derris (pbi) Bio Hexyl (pbi) Bio Friendly Pest and Disease Duster (pbi)
Dimethoate	Garden Powder (Doff) Bio Long Last (pbi) Systemic Insecticide (Doff)
Fatty acids	Safer's Fruit and Vegetable Spray (Phostrogen) Bio Friendly Pest Pistol (pbi)
Fenitrothion	Bio Fenitrothion (pbi) Garden Insect Powder (Doff)

Active ingredient	Proprietary product
● INSECTICIDES (CONTINUED)	
Gamma-HCH	Gamma-BHC Dust (Murphy) Bio Hexyl (pbi) Garden Insect Powder (Doff) Greenfly and Garden Insect Spray (Doff) Rose and Flower Spray (Secto)
Heptenophos	Tumblebug (Murphy) Systemic Action Insecticide (Murphy)
Malathion	Liquid Malathion (Murphy) Malathion Dust (Murphy) Malathion Greenfly Killer (Murphy) Bio Malathion (pbi) Bio Crop Saver (pbi)
Permethrin	Tumblebug (Murphy Systemic Action Insecticide (Murphy) Greenfly Killer (Spraydex) Picket (ICI) Bio Sprayday (pbi) Bio Crop Saver (pbi) Bio Long-Last (pbi)
Phoxim	Soil Pest Killer (Fisons)
Pirimicarb	Rapid (ICI) Rapid Aerosol (ICI)
Pirimiphos-methyl	Sybol (ICI) Sybol Soil Pest Killer (ICI) Sybol Aerosol (ICI)
Pyrethrum	Nature's Answer to Insect Pests (Fisons) Py Garden Insecticide (Vitax) Py Spray Garden Insect Killer (Vitax) Greenfly Killer (Spraydex) Greenhouse and Garden Insect Killer (Rentokil) Fruit and Vegetable Insecticide Spray (Doff) Bug Gun for Fruit and Vegetables (ICI)

Index

INDEX